NO TIME

FOR

NEUTRALITY

Discovery House PUBLISHERS

BOX 3566 · GRAND RAPIDS, MI 49501

PUBLISHING BOOKS THAT FEED THE SOUL WITH THE WORD OF GOD.

NO TIME

FOR

NEUTRALITY

A Study of Joshua

Donald K. Campbell

with
Jim Denney

Dedicated
with deep affection
and appreciation
to our children
Steve & Bobbi
Tim
Mary & Mike
Jon & Wanda

No Time for Neutrality
Copyright © 1994 Donald K. Campbell

Library of Congress Cataloging-in-Publication Data

Campbell, Donald K.
    No time for neutrality : a study of Joshua / Donald K. Campbell :
Jim Denney.
    p. cm.
    Includes bibliographical references.
    ISBN 0-929239-84-9
    1. Bible. O.T. Joshua—Criticism, interpretation, etc.
2. Leadership—Biblical teaching. 3. Joshua (Biblical figure)
I. Denney, James D. II. Title.
    BS1295.2.C352 1994
    222'.206—dc20   94-2716
                          CIP

Discovery House Publishers is affiliated with
Radio Bible Class, Grand Rapids, Michigan

Discovery House books are distributed to the trade by
Thomas Nelson Publishers, Nashville, Tennessee 37214

Printed in the United States of America

94 95 96 97 / CHG / 10 9 8 7 6 5 4 3 2 1

CONTENTS

OUTLINE OF THE BOOK OF JOSHUA

I. The Invasion of Canaan: Joshua 1:1–5:12
    A.   The Commissioning of Joshua—Joshua 1
    B.   The Spying Out of Jericho—Joshua 2
    C.   The Crossing of the Jordan—Joshua 3
    D.   The Erection of Memorials—Joshua 4
    E.   The Consecration of the People—Joshua 5:1–12

II. The Conquest of Canaan: Joshua 5:13–12:24
    A.   The Central Campaign—Joshua 6–8
    B.   The Southern Campaign—Joshua 9–10
    C.   The Northern Campaign—Joshua 11:1–15
    D.   The Review of the Victories—Joshua 11:16–12:24

III. The Division of Canaan: Joshua 13–21
    A.   The Portion of the Two-and-One-Half Tribes—Joshua 13
    B.   The Portion of Caleb—Joshua 14
    C.   The Portion of the Nine-and-One-Half Tribes—Joshua 15:1–19:48
    D.   The Portion of Joshua: the Manslayer and the Levites—Joshua 19:49–21:45

IV. Conclusion: Joshua 22–24
    A.   The Border Dispute—Joshua 22
    B.   The Last Days of Joshua—Joshua 23–24

1

FILLING THE LEADERSHIP VACUUM

Where do leaders come from?

One of our nation's most famous leaders came from the home of poor Italian immigrant parents. He started his career as a failure, at the bottom of the heap. His name was Lido.

In the late 1940s, Lido was working in fleet sales at the Chester, Pennsylvania, office of the Ford Motor Company. One day, as he was walking through the garage, his shoulders slumped and an air of dejection hovered around him. Then he heard someone calling his name. He turned and saw Charlie, his boss, approaching him. "Hey, Lido!" said Charlie, wrapping one arm about the young man's shoulders. "What are you so down about?"

"I finished thirteenth out of thirteen in sales this month, Charlie," said Lido, shaking his head. "I've gotta be the worst salesman you've got."

"Chin up, kid," said Charlie. "Somebody's gotta be last!" He clapped the young man on the back and headed for his own car. Then, over his shoulder, he called out, "But listen, Lido, just don't be last two months in a row, hear?"

Lido grinned. "I hear! I hear!"

Lido continued working hard and selling hard, and his sales figures improved. Charlie encouraged him, taught him the business, and gave him more and more responsibility. Eventually, Lido became Charlie's top salesman. Soon he was training Ford sales personnel all over the eastern seaboard.

Years passed, and Lido moved up the Ford ranks. After testing and tempering his leadership ability by developing several major vehicle lines for Ford, he was elected president of Ford in 1970. Later, he jumped from Ford to Chrysler, where, as the company's chief executive officer, he led the company from the brink of disaster ($4.75 billion in debt in 1980) to the heights of success ($925 million profit in 1983). His leadership ability is so universally admired that he has often been mentioned as candidate for the White House, and his autobiography was the best-selling non-fiction hardcover of the 1980s, with over 2 million copies sold.

By now, of course, you already know that Lido is better known to the world as Lee Iacocca, one of the most respected leaders America has produced. Though he retired as CEO of Chrysler in 1992, he is expected to have a continuing leadership role on the American business and political scene for years to come.

In America and around the world, the search is on for new, effective leaders. Young people by the hundreds are training right now to become Christian leaders of the twenty-first century. But they need models to inspire and guide them. The Bible is a rich source of such models, from Moses the liberator to David the king to Jesus the Lord to Paul the apostle to Joshua—that great Old Testament man of action. Each of these biblical models has unique strengths and character traits, and the identifying marks of Joshua—that great military genius of the Old

Testament—are his fierce loyalty to God, his forthrightness, and his courage under pressure.

Many of the leaders of our own era acknowledge that they have been instructed and inspired by the example of Joshua. General Douglas MacArthur once listed Joshua among the truly great generals of world history. And Theodore Roosevelt often said that the book of Joshua was his favorite book in the Bible. He frequently referred to Joshua in his speeches, and was no doubt motivated by the Old Testament general to be forceful, forthright, and courageous under pressure in his own position as President and leader of a nation.

Joshua arrived on the scene during a time of great crisis and opposition. The time of Joshua was no time for neutrality. It was a time when the nation of Israel was threatened by powerful military enemies without and by moral decline within. It was a time which called for *decisive action*. In other words, it was a time very much like our own perilous times.

Today, we live in a *moral crisis*. "Sin" is treated as an obsolete concept. In our culture, anything goes. In our entertainment media, in the press, in our schools and universities, and even in our government, Christian moral values are under vicious assault.

Today, we live in a *leadership crisis*. With its ballooning debt and budget deficits, the nation drifts toward economic disaster. Our current crop of leaders have proven themselves unwilling or unable to make hard but necessary decisions. Those who run our government have lost the confidence and respect of the people they are supposed to lead and serve.

Today, we live in a *social crisis*. Poverty, drugs, illiteracy, and crime soar out of control. We have lost hope of ever being able to reverse these frightening trends.

Today, we live in a *crisis of political upheaval and extremism*. Even though the Berlin wall has fallen and the Soviet Union has been dismantled, the world is still a very dangerous place. Terrorism is on the rise once again. Radical countries—and even small fanatical groups—may soon have nuclear bombs and chemical weapons. The word "peace" is always on the minds and lips of the people—and yet there is no peace.

This world cries out for leaders—forceful, forthright, courageous Christian leaders who can face the pressures of this world and persevere against opposition. This world cries out for modern-day Joshuas who can make a positive difference, bringing light and hope out of darkness and despair. The dynamic leadership model of Joshua has never been more relevant than it is *right now*, at the end of the twentieth century.

JOSHUA 1

While he was still an unknown prairie lawyer in Illinois, Abraham Lincoln was asked about his ambitions to be a political leader. He replied, "I will prepare myself and be ready. Perhaps my chance will come." In the book of Joshua, we meet another man who prepared himself and was ready: Joshua, son of Nun. As the story opens, Joshua's chance for leadership has already come.

Joshua's preparation for spiritual leadership was long, as such preparation usually is. Just as Lido "Lee" Iacocca underwent his early years of preparation under a boss named Charlie, so Joshua was prepared by his apprenticeship under a great leader named Moses. As Max DePree, CEO of Herman Miller, Inc., says in his book *Leadership is an Art*, "Leaders are . . . responsible for future leadership. They need to identify, develop, and nurture future leaders."[1] Moses was a leader who took this responsibility seriously—and we should too.

The ancient Jewish historian Josephus believed Joshua to be about 40 years old at the time of the Exodus, when Moses led the Israelites out of Egypt. As the book of Joshua opens, Moses is dead and Joshua is about 80. God's preparation of this man is complete. Joshua is ready to succeed Moses, and to take on the task of leading the nation of Israel.

This should be an encouragement to all of us who aspire to a leadership role in some arena of life. We live in an age of impatience, and many people in their forties, or thirties, or even their twenties, are saying, "I should be in this position or in that leadership role by now! I should be farther along in my career or my ministry! Why haven't my abilities been recognized? Why haven't my achievements been rewarded?"

The example of Joshua should be instructive and encouraging to those of us who feel impatient with our career path or our ministry path. Wherever we are in life, we are in a place where character can be built, where skills can be honed, where new knowledge and wisdom can be acquired. We may feel that God isn't even using us right now, but God has a plan for us. He is preparing us for the challenges ahead, just as he prepared Joshua during the first eight decades of his life.

The New Leader

Leadership transitions often occur in times of crisis. In fact, crises are often *precipitated* when a leader suddenly dies or resigns. I vividly remember the moment in April 1945 when, as a college student, I heard the chilling words, "F.D.R. is dead!" Hearing those words, I anxiously wondered if Vice President Harry Truman could pick up the mantle of the fallen President and lead America to victory in World War II. Truman's leadership abilities had never been tested, and though the war in Europe was winding down, it appeared the war in the Pacific could last another year, if not several years. Despite the doubts that existed in 1945, today we look back on Truman as one of our greatest leaders.

Eighteen years after the death of F.D.R., the nation was again stunned by the death of a President. Another eleven years passed, and the nation suddenly lost another leader—this time when President Nixon resigned. The loss of a leader creates a vacuum. As a new leader steps into that vacuum, people always wonder, "Can he do it? Is he up to the job?" A mood of crisis and doubt prevails.

The leadership transition from Moses to Joshua was equally momentous. Many people probably wondered if Joshua would be an able successor to the legendary Moses. And, from a purely human viewpoint, Joshua performed his leadership role with distinction and even brilliance. In today's terms, he was Patton, MacArthur, and Stormin' Norman Schwarzkopf rolled into one!

But the book of Joshua gives us an even more elevated perspective. Joshua was more than just a great military strategist. He was a man who knew how to listen to the *real* Leader of Israel—Jehovah Himself. Though Moses was dead, God was alive, and it was God himself who now communicated directly with Joshua.

Joshua Listens to the Lord (1:1–9)

Joshua waited expectantly near the swiftly flowing Jordan River to hear the voice of God—and he was not disappointed. When God's servants take time to listen, He always communicates. In our time, God speaks through His written Word and through the still, small voice of His Spirit. But back then, God spoke in a dream by night, or in a vision by day, or through the high priest of the tabernacle, or by an audible voice.

In whatever way God chose to communicate with Joshua, the message came through loud and clear: though Moses was dead, God's purpose was very much alive, and Joshua was now the key figure in the fulfillment of God's program. As William S. LaSor observes,

> God expects each generation to get up on its own feet and face its own problems. God does not want us to stand around saying, "Well, now, look at Moses. *There* was a great man! We will never have another man like Moses!" . . . Moses is dead. Great man that he was, he is dead. Get up and face the problems of your day and your age! Arise, go over this Jordan. Do not long for the past. Do the work of the present, and God says, "I will be with you."[2]

That was the attitude of Joshua, and it should be our attitude as well as we face the leadership challenges of our own time. What is the leadership vacuum God is calling you to fill today? What is the important task that remains unfinished because no one has accepted responsibility for that task? What is the leadership role God is calling you to fill right now in your family? In your business? In your church? In your community? In your country? In your world?

These are the same kinds of questions that confronted Joshua. He looked at the leadership vacuum left by the death of Moses, his mentor, and listened for the voice of God. And God described the task he now set before Joshua, and gave him clear instructions in how to carry out that task: Joshua was to assume immediate command of all the people and lead them across the Jordan and into the land of Canaan.

In the centuries since Joshua's time, many nations have challenged Israel's right to the land which God was about to give them. But no one can question God's right to give Canaan to Israel, for He owns all the lands of Planet Earth. "The earth is the Lord's and all it contains, the world, and those that dwell in it" (Ps. 24:1).

Although the land was God's gift to Israel, it would only be won by hard fighting. In verses 3 and 4, God told Joshua that he gave the Israelite's title to the territory — but they could possess it only by marching on every part of it. The boundaries were to extend from the wilderness on the south to the Lebanon mountain range on the north; and from the Euphrates River on the east to the Mediterranean Sea on the west.

When Joshua heard these words, his heart must have skipped a beat or two! Thirty-eight years before, as one of the twelve spies sent by Moses, he had walked through this good and fruitful land (see Numbers 13). Even after all those years, the memory of the beauty and fertility of Canaan was not dimmed. Now Joshua was to lead the armies of Israel into Canaan to conquer and possess the land.

A Promise That Still Awaits Fulfillment

The territory actually conquered and possessed by Israel under Joshua's leadership was much less than the land God promised to Joshua in chapter 1. In verse 4, God promised Israel a piece of real estate that covers not only modern-day Israel, but large portions of Lebanon, Syria, Jordan, and Iraq as well! During the time of David and Solomon, when the land of Israel reached its greatest extent, the outlying districts of the land Joshua was promised were within Israel's sphere of influence—*but not under its rule.* To this day, God's promise to Joshua still awaits complete fulfillment.

When will the nation of Israel fully possess the land?

A step toward fulfillment of this promise took place in our own century. In November 1947, 56 delegates to the United Nations met in Flushing, New York, to decide the future of Israel. As the delegate from Guatemala rose to cast the first vote, a piercing cry came from the spectators' gallery—a cry as old as the suffering of the Hebrew people: *"Ana Ad Hoshija!"* "O Lord, save us!" The results of the vote: 33 in favor of establishing the state of Israel, 10 against, and 13 abstaining.

Jews danced in the streets of New York, Philadelphia, Sao Paulo, London, Paris, and Tel Aviv. In Jerusalem, Golda Meir said, "We have waited 2,000 years for our deliverance." David Ben-Gurion whispered in awe, "At last we are a free people."

But Palestine was still a divided land and Jerusalem a divided city. Not until 1967 was Israel able to expand her territory and unify the city of Jerusalem. But even then, Israel was far from occupying all the land God promised to Joshua. Today, tremendous pressures are being exerted upon Israel to return much of her conquered territory to Arab control in return for promises of peace. The pressures and opposition against Israel will certainly continue until they climax at the time of Christ's return to earth, when He will deliver the Jews and reign in the land, the undisputed King of a converted and redeemed Israel. When that glorious day comes, the promise to Joshua will be fulfilled.

There is a lesson for us in the unrealized promise to Joshua. The reason that promise remains unfulfilled is not that God has failed to keep his side of the bargain, but because apathy, unbelief, and disobedience kept the people under Joshua from claiming all that God wanted to give them. In the same way, we Christians all too often fall short of appropriating the spiritual blessings God has provided for us now in Christ. As Ephesians 1:3 tells us, we Christians are blessed with "every spiritual blessing in the heavenly places in Christ"—but like the Israelites in Joshua's day, we possess only what we appropriate by faith and obedience.

A Three-Fold Call to Courage

As Joshua faced the tremendous task of conquering Canaan, he desperately needed a word of encouragement. Joshua knew that the Canaanites were vigorous people who lived in strongly fortified cities. Frequent battles kept their warriors in trim fighting condition. Most of their land was rugged and mountainous—a fact which would make war maneuvers very difficult for the Israelite army.

But God never gives a command without a promise. He assured Joshua of a lifetime of continuous victory over his enemies, based on His unfailing presence and power. The promise in verse 5, "I will not fail you or forsake you," may be translated, "I will not drop you or abandon you," or even, "I will not leave you in the lurch." God never walks out on His promises.

Flowing from this strong affirmation came a three-fold call to courage:

Call to Courage No. 1: In verse 6, God calls Joshua to be strong and courageous because of *the promise of the land.* Although he would need strength and fortitude for the strenuous military campaign ahead, Joshua was to keep uppermost in his mind the fact that he would succeed in bringing Israel into its inheritance because the land had been promised to "their fathers" as an eternal possession—that is, to Abraham (see Gen. 13:14ff; 15:18ff; 17:7ff), to Isaac (see Gen. 26:3ff); to Jacob (see

Gen. 28:13; 35:12), and to the entire nation, the seed of Abraham (see Ex. 6:8).

At last, Joshua was to lead the sons of Israel into possession of the Promised Land. What a strategic role he would play in a critical time in the history of Israel!

The fulfillment of God's promise of this land to the people of Israel depends—in any given generation—on Israel's obedience to God. There can be no question, however, that Israel has a God-given legal right to the land, because God affirms that right repeatedly in His Word! By divine contract, the title to the land belongs to the people of Israel—even though they will not possess it totally and enjoy it fully until, as a people, they are right with God.

Call to Courage No. 2: In verse 7, God calls Joshua to be strong and courageous because of *the power of the Word of God.* This exhortation is stronger than that of verse 6, indicating that it takes more strength of character to obey God's Word than to win military battles! These verses clearly speak of a written body of truth. Although critics argue that the Scriptures did not appear in written form until several centuries later, we read here of an authoritative "Book of the Law."

In verse 8, God told Joshua that if he wanted prosperity and success in the conquest of Canaan—and there is no question that he did!—he needed to observe the following:

• The Law was not to depart out of his mouth; he was to talk about it continually.

• He was to meditate on it day and night; he was to think about it continually.

• He was to obey its commands; he was to live according to it and keep it conscientiously.

The record of Joshua's life, as told in the Books of Exodus through Joshua, demonstrates that he did indeed live according to the teachings of the Law of Moses. This alone explains the victories he achieved in battle and the success with which his entire career was marked. In one of his farewell addresses to the nation just prior to his death, he urged the people also to live their lives in submission to God's Word (see Josh. 23:6). Joshua's generation heeded this counsel, but later generations abandoned it. Instead of ordering their lives by God's authoritative revelation, they chose instead to do what was right in their own eyes (see Jud. 21:25). Rejecting an objective standard of righteousness, they chose to follow their own desires, appetites, and inclinations—a situation not unlike the moral and spiritual relativism of our own day. That tragic choice led Israel into centuries of religious apostasy, moral anarchy, and the loss of their own land and freedom.

What about our own society, with its moral permissiveness and the present upsurge in cults, the occult, and apostate distortions of Christianity? Could our society be headed for a fate similar to that which awaited an apostate Israel? Many authorities, both religious and secular, think so. If we are honest, we have to admit that we already live in a post-Christian age, and that America is no longer "one nation under God." Western civilization has largely rejected the authority of Scripture, opting instead for moral and spiritual relativism. As former Chief Justice Frederick M. Vinson once said, "Nothing is more certain in modern society than the principle that there are no absolutes." In other words, the only absolute is that there are *no* absolutes!

Pick up any newspaper or click on CNN. The evidence stares you in the face: We are witnessing the death of biblical values in our culture. As Francis Schaeffer observed,

> Humanists have been determined to beat to death
> the knowledge of God and the knowledge that God has
> not been silent, but has spoken in the Bible and through
> Christ—and they have been determined to do this, even
> though the death of values has come with the death of
> that knowledge.[3]

As biblical values are put to death in our society, our
society itself begins to die. The most important values of
our culture used to be family, loyalty, honesty, honor,
and sacrifice. Today, however, these values have been
replaced by slogans such as "freedom of choice" and
"express yourself" and "I'm worth it."

In many parts of our country, school children can be
taught a variety of sex acts in graphic detail, then they
can be given condoms and free abortions without parental consent—but the same laws which mandate these
abuses of our children also forbid teaching abstinence to
those children, *even as one of several options!* Why?
Because biblical values are rejected, and everyone does
what is right in his own eyes.

Our tax money goes to support the production of "art"
which in one case represented Jesus Christ on the cross—
submerged in a jar of urine! Those who protest this kind of
assault on Christian sensibilities are accused of "bigotry"
and "censorship." Why? Because biblical values are
rejected, and everyone does what is right in his own eyes.

Over a million human lives are destroyed every year
in the name of "choice." Those who oppose abortion on
moral grounds are vilified by the press and told by their
own government officials to "end their love affair with the
fetus." Why? Because values are dead, and everyone
does what is right in their own eyes.

Joshua believed—and so must we—that there is a
God to whom we must give account, a God who has

revealed Himself and His will for us in the Holy Scriptures. True prosperity and success for the individual and the nation come only by following His teachings.

Call to Courage No. 3: In verse 9, God calls Joshua to be strong and courageous because of *the promised presence of the Lord.* Joshua faced an enormous task. He would have to wrest control of the land from battle-seasoned armies within heavily fortified cities! But the presence of God would make all the difference. As Martin Luther said, "One plus God equals a majority!"

Joshua probably experienced times when he felt weak and inadequate, when the task seemed too formidable to begin, much less accomplish. But God, knowing that times of fear and discouragement lay ahead for Joshua, said to him three times, "Be strong and of good courage." These words of command, coupled with God's strong assurances and dependable promises, were sufficient to last Joshua a lifetime.

And they are sufficient for you and me.

Joshua Commands His Officers (1:10–15)

The Lord had spoken to Joshua. Now Joshua spoke to the people—and he did so without delay. There was a note of confidence and certainty in Joshua's commands. The new leader was a "take-charge" kind of man.

Joshua and the people faced a situation that closely paralleled the dilemma Moses and the Israelites faced at the Red Sea (Ex. 14). In each case, the obstacle occurred at the beginning of the leader's ministry. Both were impossible to solve though natural means. Both demanded unconditional dependence upon a miracle-working, all-powerful God.

Two matters had to be settled before the march across the Jordan began: (1) provisions had to be gathered; and (2) an attack force had to be assembled. Israel had three days in which to accomplish these two goals.

The gathering of provisions took place in a very systematic way, through a chain of command. The order was issued by Joshua to his officers, who then issued the orders of Commander Joshua to the people. Though the daily manna continued to appear for the nation of Israel, the people were still required to gather some of the fruit and grain from the plains of Moab to feed both themselves and their cattle.

The second order of business—the assembling of the attack force—took place by Joshua's direct order. He reminded the tribes of Reuben, Gad, and the half-tribe of Manasseh of their commitment to assist in conquering the land west of Jordan. Although they had already received their inheritance on the east side of the Jordan (the region called Transjordan), their response showed they were ready to stand by their promise. Joshua had a special mission for these Transjordanian tribes—to serve as shock troops in leading the attack on Canaan.

Joshua Receives Support from the People (1:16–18)

The response of the tribes of Transjordan was enthusiastic and wholehearted, and no doubt a profound encouragement to Joshua. Their pledge of loyalty and obedience included the solemn declaration that anyone guilty of disobedience would be executed.

But there was one condition (verse 17): they were willing to follow Joshua *provided he show clear evidence that he was led by God*. This was a wise precaution and one that all of the Lord's people should follow today! Otherwise, they may find their leaders to be "blind leaders of the blind." Those who follow the wise precaution of the Transjordanian tribes, who demand evidence that their leaders are led by God, need not fear the same fate as the 900 cult followers of Jim Jones, who died in the jungles of Guyana in 1978. Nor do they need fear the same fate as the scores of cult followers of Vernon Howell (a.k.a. "David Koresh"), who died in their blazing compound outside Waco, Texas, in 1993.

Joshua was no "blind leader of the blind." The hand of God was upon him all his days, and with faith in the Lord he moved boldly forward to lead the people in the conquest of the land of promise. What was the secret of Joshua's success as a leader? We find it in verse 8: "This Book of the Law shall not depart from your mouth; but you shall meditate on it day and night, so that you may be careful to do according to all that is written in it; for then you will make your way prosperous, and then you will have success."

You may say, "But that's no secret! What I'm looking for is hidden power, a magic formula to transform my life!" To this attitude, Alan Redpath replies,

> I have no magic formula for your holiness; I have no hocus-pocus treatment to offer you; I have no short-cut to spiritual power for any of you. All I can do is to say to you: Get back to your Bible; "meditate therein day and night," and go down before God on your face in prayer. For the greatest transactions of a man's experience are made, not in a church, but behind closed doors.[4]

Here is the first "secret" of godly leadership that we learn from the example of Joshua: *A true Christian leader maintains continual fellowship with God—not only in public, but in private, where nobody else sees.* He talks to God. He listens to God. He searches God's Word for insight and guidance. Then, when he goes forth to lead, he goes with the courage and confidence that comes from knowing he is following the course that God has prepared for him.

Some years ago, the newly elected CEO of one of our nation's largest insurance companies spoke these words before the entire staff of his company's headquarters:

> I have some deep spiritual and religious convictions that I've tried to make part of my life. I have a very deep consciousness of the overriding providence of God in the affairs of men. I don't believe that our civilization is automatic. I don't believe our country's blessings are automatic. I don't believe the great prosperity of this company is automatic. I believe we are subject to the overruling providence of God in the affairs of our lives, and I can tell you in these last few days that I spent a lot of time in thankful prayer to God for what He has brought to pass in my life.[5]

When Moses was dead and Joshua stepped into the leadership vacuum, he immediately inspired confidence. And he did so not merely because he was a man of bold courage, nor because he was able to speak with dynamic power, nor merely because he was a selflessly committed leader. When he spoke and said, "Follow me into the land of promise," the people responded and followed because they knew that God was with him, just as God had been with Moses.

Joshua inspired confidence in his leadership because he was a leader who listened to God. May others see God in us, speaking through us, leading us, calling us onward as we serve Him in every arena of our lives.

QUESTIONS FOR REFLECTION AND DISCUSSION

Note: The questions at the end of each chapter in this book have been designed to help you apply the principles of Joshua's life to all the areas of leadership in your own life. They are designed to make this material more meaningful either in your own private study or in a small discussion group study, such as a Sunday school or home Bible study group.

The questions are divided into three sections. The first section, *See Your Own Reflection*, is designed to help you identify with the Bible passage and see how the dynamics of your own life are reflected in the life of Joshua. The second section, *Dig a Little Deeper*, is designed to help you wrestle with the issues and the content of Joshua's story. The final section, *Let's Get Personal*, is intended to help you apply the truths and principles of Joshua's story to your own life in a personal, practical way.

We hope this study enriches your understanding of the leadership model of Joshua, and helps you to build character strengths and spiritual disciplines which will last a lifetime and bring eternal honor to God.

DISCOVERY HOUSE PUBLISHERS

See Your Own Reflection

1. Who has been a "Moses," a mentor, to you? What is the most important leadership lesson you have learned from that person?

Dig a Little Deeper

2. How do you think God spoke to Joshua? Through a vision? An audible voice? How do you picture the scene in verses 1 through 9? How does God speak to you today?

3. In verse 7, God commands Joshua to be strong, courageous, and faithful to God's law—and promises that the result of Joshua's faithfulness will be "success." How do you think God defines "success"? What does this promise really mean?

4. Read the promises God makes to Joshua in verses 3–5 and 9. Which of these promises is the most meaningful in your life right now?

Let's Get Personal

5. What kind of pressure or opposition are you facing today?

6. Do you feel your life is "on hold," that you are in a "waiting mode"? Does the eighty-year time of preparation that Joshua went through encourage you? Why or why not?

7. As Dr. Campbell asks in this chapter, "What is the leadership vacuum God is calling you to fill right now? What is the important task that remains unfinished because no one has accepted responsibility for that task? What is the leadership role God is calling you to fill *right now* in your family? In your business? In your church? In your community? In your country? In your world?"

2

LIVING IN ENEMY TERRITORY

JOSHUA 2

Elie Cohn has been called Israel's greatest spy. In the 1960s, he infiltrated the highest echelons of the Syrian government, gaining access to vital military secrets. He even toured military installations on the Syrian-Israeli border, where he learned the defense plans, the attack plans, and the location of armaments and fortifications. All of this information he reported to Israel by a transmitter from a hidden location in Damascus. Though he was living deep in enemy territory and literally rubbing elbows with the sworn enemies of his people, Elie Cohn played a major role in Israel's most outstanding victories during the historic Six Day War in 1967.

This dramatic story was foreshadowed over three thousand years earlier by the thrilling adventure of the two spies who were sent by Joshua into the enemy-held land of Canaan. In Joshua 2, we find the account of how these spies penetrated a Canaanite city and brought back vital information to their commander, Joshua.

Even in this high-tech age of AWACS planes, satellite reconnaissance, remotely piloted vehicles, and "stealth" technology, effective military intelligence still requires living, breathing people sneaking behind enemy lines, living in enemy territory, ferreting out enemy secrets at close range. Some people think that the Gulf War of 1991 was a "push-button" war, a war won by missiles and radars and computers. But the truth is that the generals of the U.N. forces relied very heavily on information relayed from spies and soldiers who were on the ground, deep in enemy territory, acquiring information with their own eyes and ears and relaying it electronically back to Allied Forces headquarters in Riyadh, Saudi Arabia.

As Bible scholar George Hague notes,

> It is well known that the function of the spy in war is a dangerous one; yet it is absolutely necessary. Everything depends on the commander of an army having accurate intelligence of the position and movement of the enemy, if they are in the field; or of the strength, character, and position of the fortification, if it is a city that is to be attacked. The work of a spy demands great courage, coolness, adroitness, and resource. If he is found out, he is shot without mercy.[1]

When Joshua sent out his spies, he knew both the hazards they would be facing and the valuable information they could retrieve. He, too, had once lived the life of a spy. As he faced westward and surveyed the land that God had promised, a land which lay just across the turbulent waters of the Jordan, it was only natural and prudent that he should take steps to secure the kind of quality information needed to ensure the success of the opening battle of a long and difficult war.

The Spies are Sent to Jericho (2:1)

The walled city of Jericho stood directly in the path of the Israeli invasion. It was the key citadel of the Jordan

Valley, and it commanded the passes into the central highlands. Before his army attacked, Joshua needed complete information concerning this fortress—its gates, its fortified towers, its military forces, and the morale of its people.

So Joshua selected two secret agents and sent them on a carefully concealed mission. Not even the Israelites were to know about this spy mission. He didn't want an unfavorable report to dishearten the people, as it had discouraged their fathers at Kadesh-barnea. (See Num. 13:28–14:4.)

Taking their lives in their hands, the two spies left Shittim, about six miles east of the Jordan River. They probably traveled north until they could find a place to swim across or ford the flooded river. Turning south, they approached Jericho from the north as if they were mere Canaanite travelers. Soon, they were walking the very streets of Jericho, mingling with its people, observing its fortifications—and preparing for its downfall.

How did the spies happen to choose the house of Rahab the prostitute as their base and their place of refuge? The Scripture passage does not tell us. One inference we should definitely *not* draw from this passage is that the spies visited Rahab with any immoral purposes in mind. As Bible commentator William Blaikie observes,

> The emissaries of Joshua were in too serious peril, in too devout a mood, and in too high-strung a state of nerve to be at the mercy of any Delilah that might wish to lure them to careless pleasure. Their faith, their honor, their patriotism, and their regard to their leader Joshua, all demanded the extremest circumspection and self-control; they were, like Peter, walking on the sea; unless they kept their eye on their Divine Protector, their courage and presence of mind would fail them; they would be at the mercy of their foes.[2]

Some Bible scholars suggest that the spies simply saw Rahab walking the streets and followed her back to her house. I believe, however, that God, through some sort of divine inner leading, brought these men to her house. God had a mission for these two spies that even they did not imagine—a mission that included more than merely obtaining military information. Rahab was a sinful woman living in a sinful city, but God in his grace had chosen to spare her from the judgment that was about to fall upon Jericho. So, in his mysterious and all-wise way, the Lord brought together these two Israelite secret agents and this prostitute from Canaan. Soon, the prostitute would become a *proselyte*, a committed follower and worshiper of the Holy God of Israel.

Historians from the time of Josephus unto the present day have attempted to gloss over or explain away the immoral nature of Rahab's line of work. Some have suggested that she wasn't really a prostitute, but merely an innkeeper. But both the language of the Old Testament and references in the New Testament (Heb. 11:31 and James 2:25) make it clear that she was indeed a prostitute, a woman who supported herself in an immoral way.

Does this fact somehow impugn the righteousness of God? Has God somehow erred in using such a conspicuously sinful woman to further His plan? Absolutely not! God in His sovereignty and His grace can use anyone and anything to achieve his purposes. Jesus called to Himself tax collectors and sinners; He showed grace to these people and He used them to further His eternal purpose. In the book of Acts, God called to Himself a brutal, hardened Pharisee, a persecutor of Christians named Paul— and through Paul, God produced roughly a third of the New Testament! In Numbers 22, God even caused a *donkey* to speak in order to achieve his plan! God can use donkeys, prostitutes, tax collectors, and Pharisees to achieve his goals if He so chooses. That is the kind of God we serve. The challenge before you and me is to heed the example of Rahab, to respond to God's grace as willingly and eagerly as she did, and to become partners with God in His grand design for human history.

The Spies are Shielded by Rahab (2:2–7)

Verses 2 through 7 shows the tremendous danger these spies were in and the tense state of alert which gripped the city of Jericho. The military authorities of the city knew that the vast population of Israel was camped opposite Jericho, across the Jordan River. Even though the agents managed to enter the city undetected, something gave them away—perhaps something about their physical appearance, their dress, or their speech. The Canaanite person who detected them as secret agents also followed them to Rahab's house, then rushed to report the discovery to the king. The king immediately sent messengers who demanded that Rahab surrender the spies. In keeping with the customs of the Middle East, the king's messengers respected the privacy of even an ill-reputed woman such as Rahab. There was no attempt to burst into her house to prosecute their search.

Rahab had her own suspicions about the identity of the two visitors. When she saw the soldiers approaching her house, she hid the spies beneath the stalks of flax which were drying on her flat roof.

When she opened her front door to the king's messengers, she freely admitted that two strangers had come to her house, but she claimed to have no idea who they were or what their mission was. "They left here at dusk," she said, "just about the time the city gate is closed. But if you hurry you can probably catch them!" The soldiers took Rahab at her word, made no search of her property, and quickly set out on a wild-goose chase due east to the fords of the Jordan, the most likely escape route.

Was it wrong for Rahab to lie, since her falsehood protected the spies? Are there some situations in which a lie is acceptable?

Some say this was a cultural matter, for Rahab was born and raised among the depraved Canaanites who thought nothing of lying. She probably saw no evil in her act. Further, if she had told the truth, the spies would surely have been killed by the king of Jericho.

But such arguments are not fully convincing. Erwin Lutzer describes a situation which logically seemed to call for lying, but which in the end brought worse results than would have come from the truth. He writes,

> Several years ago, the State Department lied about the U-2 spy plane incident. This may have been done out of love for 180 million Americans, because their trust in the honesty of the government is crucial. Also it preserved good relations with Russia and kept a military secret which was necessary to insure future security measures. Although the original explanation by the State Department was plausible, the lie was discovered. This resulted in greater hatred among nations, and the confidence of many Americans was lost.[3]

To argue that the spies would certainly have perished if Rahab had been truthful is to ignore the option that God could have protected the spies in some other way. To excuse Rahab for indulging in a common practice is to condone what God condemns. Paul quoted a poet of Crete who said that Cretans were inveterate liars, and then added, "This testimony is true. For this cause reprove them severely that they may be sound in the faith" (Titus 1:13). The lie of Rahab was recorded but not approved. The Bible approves her faith, demonstrated by good works—but it does not condone her lie.

The Spies Gather Intelligence Information (2:8–11)

After the king's messengers left, Rahab climbed to the roof of her home where she talked with the two spies in the darkness. They could hardly have been prepared to hear this Canaanite prostitute declare her faith in their own God!

First, she disclosed that she believed that the Lord, the God of Israel, had given them the land of Canaan. Though the army of Israel had not yet crossed the Jordan River, Rahab said, in effect, "I can see that the conquest is as good as accomplished." Rahab intuitively sensed which side was going to be victorious.

Second, she revealed the priceless information to the spies that the inhabitants of Jericho, as well the inhabitants of the rest of Canaan, were utterly demoralized. Since a major objective of the spy mission was to assess the morale of the enemy, this word came as welcome news!

But *why* were these Canaanites so afraid of Israel? Because of the power of Israel's God! The story of how the Lord parted the Red Sea for these Hebrew slaves some forty years earlier had spread from Egypt into the land of Canaan. More recently, the Israelite army had also gained victory over the mighty kings of the Amorites, Sihon and Og, in the land east of the Jordan (Num. 21). The Canaanites knew that the same divine power which had destroyed the armies of the Egyptians and the Amorites was now being aimed at them—and they knew they could not resist.

Rahab knew better than to believe that a nation of former slaves could have achieved such legendary victories by their own strength. She clearly understood that behind these Israelites who were camped across the river stood an invisible but invincible Power—Jehovah, the God of the Hebrews. Common sense told her it was useless to resist this God and His people, so she threw in her lot with the two spies from Israel.

In verse 11, Rahab said, "For the Lord your God, He is God in heaven above and on earth beneath." Responding to the word she had received about the mighty works of God, Rahab believed. She trusted in God's power and mercy—

And it was her *faith* that saved her.

The Spies Promise to Protect Rahab (2:12–21)

Not only did Rahab demonstrate her faith by the protection of the spies, but also by her concern for the safety of her family. Admittedly, it was their *physical* deliverance she sought. But it may well be that she also sensed her own *spiritual* need and the spiritual need of her family. She saw a faith and a confidence in these Hebrew spies that she had never seen in the men of her own culture. Arrogance, violence, abusiveness—yes, she had seen that before, but these men of Israel were different. She wanted to have that difference in her own life, and in the lives of the people she loved. She wanted for herself and her family to become part of God's family, serving the one true God of Israel instead of being enslaved by the vile and degrading idolatry of the Canaanites. Rahab pursued this urgent issue delicately, but persistently. She pressed the spies to make a pact with her in consideration of the cooperation and protection she had shown them.

In asking the spies to show "kindness" to her family, she used a significant and meaningful word, *hesed*. This word is found some 250 times in the Old Testament, and it means loyal, steadfast, or faithful love based on an unwritten promise or agreement. Sometimes, the word is used for God's covenant love for His people; and sometimes, as here, for relationships on the human level. Rahab's request, then, was that the spies make a *hesed* agreement with her and her father's house, just as she had made a *hesed* agreement with them by sparing their lives.

The response of the spies was immediate and decisive. "When the Lord gives us the land, we will keep the *hesed* agreement. If you do not report our mission, we will protect you and your family or forfeit our own lives!" (See verse 14.)

As the spies prepared to go, they again confirmed the pact by repeating and enlarging the conditions Rahab must abide by:

• First, her house must be designated by a scarlet cord hung from the window. Because of the position of the house on the outer wall of the city of Jericho, the cord would be clearly seen by the Israelite soldiers again and again as they marched around the walls. Her home would be clearly marked so that no soldier—however fierce and eager to carry out his orders to destroy the city—would dare violate the oath and kill the inhabitants of the house.

• Second, Rahab and her family were to remain in the house during the attack on Jericho. If any of them wandered out and was killed, the responsibility for his death would be his own.

• Finally, the spies again emphasized that they would be free of this oath of protection if Rahab exposed their mission.

We can easily imagine Rahab hurrying to gather her family in her house on the city wall. The door of her house was a door to safety and refuge from the judgment which was about to fall upon Jericho.

In the days of Noah, there was safety and refuge for those who entered into the door of the ark. In Egypt, there was safety and refuge for those who were gathered behind the doors that were sprinkled with the blood of the Passover lamb. For you and me, there is safety and refuge from eternal judgment—but only if we enter the right door: Jesus Christ alone. As He said in John 10:9, "I am the door; if anyone enters through Me, he shall be saved."

George Whitefield, the eloquent preacher of the Great Awakening in North America (1738–40), once spoke on the text, "The Door Was Shut." There were two arrogant and disrespectful young men in the congregation, and one was overheard to say to the other in mocking tones, "What if the door is shut? Another will open!"

Later in the sermon, the evangelist said, "It is possible that there may be someone here who is careless and self–satisfied, and says, 'What does it matter if the door is shut? Another will open!' "

The two young men looked at each other in alarm!

"Yes, another door will open," Whitefield concluded. "It will be the door to the bottomless pit—the door to hell!"

There is only one door to eternal life, and the name of that door is Jesus Christ.

The Spies Return to Joshua (2:22–24)

Jericho was surrounded by two massive walls—an inner wall and an outer wall, set about fifteen feet apart. Planks of wood were set atop the two walls, spanning the gap. Because space was at a premium in the small city, houses were then built on this foundation of wooden planks. These houses, which were exposed atop the walls instead of enjoying the protection of being within the walls, were the homes of the poorer and less reputable citizens of Jericho. Prostitutes such as Rahab certainly fell within this category.

Once the spies' mission was completed, Rahab lowered the two men down the outer wall by a rope from a window of her house (verse 15). Then Rahab and the spies exchanged parting instructions (verses 16 through 21); the spies departed and Rahab fastened the scarlet cord in her window. No doubt, the spies could never have escaped through the city gate, since the king was alerted and the gate was being carefully watched.

Leaving the city, the spies headed for the hill country—an area scarcely a half-mile west of Jericho. Their departure from the city was apparently observed, probably by guards along the walls. Soldiers from the city pursued them into the hill country. In that region, there are limestone cliffs about 1,500 feet high, honeycombed with caves. There the spies hid for three days until the soldiers gave up the hunt.

Then, under the cover of darkness, the spies swam back across the Jordan, making their way quickly back to the camp at Shittim, to present their report to Joshua. How excited they must have been to be able to deliver such a favorable report! They eagerly related their adventure and their findings to Joshua—and especially the fearful and demoralized state of the enemy. "Surely the Lord has given all the land into our hands," they concluded, "and all the inhabitants of the land, moreover, have melted away before us."

How different was this report from the report of the majority of spies at Kadesh-barnea, who said, "We are not able to go up against the people, for they are too strong for us" (Num. 13:31)! Undoubtedly, Joshua received this new and favorable report with rejoicing and gratitude to God. Early the next morning, he organized the army of Israel for the attack on Jericho.

Faith to Stand Alone Against a Hostile World

While the courage and exploits of the two Israelite spies should not be minimized, it is Rahab who truly "steals the scene" and rivets our attention in Joshua chapter 2. Whenever she is spoken of in the Bible, she is referred to as a "harlot" or prostitute. This is not done to humiliate her or to demean her memory, but to highlight the amazing grace of God—grace sufficient to transform a prostitute into a full-fledged partner in the eternal plan of God. Regardless of the kind of life a person has lived, there is forgiveness for sin and eternal life available through Jesus Christ.

We see a similar contrast between the old life and the new, grace-transformed life in the story of an eighteenth century man named John Newton. Losing his mother when he was seven years old, Newton went to sea at the age of eleven. "I went to Africa," he said, "that I might be free to sin to my heart's content." And that he did!

During the next few years, Newton's soul was seared by the most revolting of all human experiences. He fell into the cruel hands of a "press-gang"—one of those roving bands of "Royal Navy recruiters" who used to scour the waterfront taverns and brothels for "recruits" for His Majesty's Navy. These "press-gangs" often persuaded their "volunteers" to join the Navy with a blow to the head from a club. Newton's own career in the Navy was short and violent. He deserted, was captured and flogged until his back was raw and bloody, then deserted again.

He joined the African slave trade, where he became not only a witness but a participant in unspeakable atrocities against his fellow human beings. Going from bad to worse, he eventually became a slave himself, finally being sold in bondage to a woman slave. She gloried in her power over Newton, making him depend for his food on the crusts she tossed under her table. In the epitaph Newton composed for himself, he called himself "the slave of slaves."

And then it happened! In 1748, on board a ship about to founder in the grip of a storm, the Lord came from on high and delivered him out of deep waters. When the ship went plunging down into the trough of the seas, few on board expected her to come up again. As Newton hurried to the pumps, he said to the captain, "If this will not do, the Lord have mercy upon us!" His own words startled him. "Mercy!" he said to himself in astonishment. "Mercy! Mercy!" On the 10th of March 1748, Newton sought mercy—and found it!

Somehow, the ship survived the storm. When it reached port, Newton left the slave trade and became one of the greatest preachers and hymn writers in Christian history. He poured his own story into the words of his best-known hymn:

> Amazing grace! How sweet the sound
>   That saved a wretch like me!
> I once was lost, but now am found,
>   Was blind, but now I see!

In Joshua 2, we see this same amazing grace at work in the life of an ancient Canaanite prostitute. The Bible emphasizes not only that Rahab was saved by faith, but also that she demonstrated her faith by her works: She protected the spies. She dropped the scarlet cord from her window. She gathered her family in her house to protect them from the judgment that was to fall on Jericho. Rahab took her life in her hands to protect the spies. She believed God even though she had limited knowledge of Him. As the writer to the Hebrews said,

> Without faith, it is impossible to please Him, for he who comes to God must believe that He is, and that He is a rewarder of those who seek Him. . . . By faith Rahab the harlot did not perish along with those who were disobedient, after she had welcomed the spies in peace.[4]

Rahab demonstrated her faith in the most dramatic and convincing way possible: She risked her own life! As Francis Schaeffer expressed it,

> This woman Rahab stood alone in faith against the *total* culture which surrounded her—something none of us today in the Western world has ever yet had to do. For a period of time she stood for the unseen against the seen, standing in acute danger until Jericho fell. If the king had ever found out what she had done, he would have become her chief enemy and would have executed her. . . . This is exactly how the Christian lives, and Rahab is a tremendous example for us. Though you and I have stepped from the kingdom of darkness into the kingdom of God's dear Son, we are still surrounded by a culture controlled by God's great enemy, Satan. We must live in it from the moment we accept Christ as Saviour until judgment falls. We too are encompassed by one who was once our king but is now our enemy. It is just plain stupid of a Christian not to expect spiritual warfare while he lives in enemy territory.[5]

Like Rahab, we are all called by God to take a stand—sometimes a very lonely stand—against a hostile world. Living in enemy territory is dangerous and demands a vital faith in the living God. Rahab possessed such a faith—and she demonstrated it.

Do you?

QUESTIONS FOR REFLECTION AND DISCUSSION

See Your Own Reflection

1. What is the most daring thing you have ever done?

Dig a Little Deeper

2. Put yourself in the spies' position. You have just made it into the enemy city. You notice that a few people are giving you curious looks. And that sneaky-looking fellow over there! Is he following you? You need a place to hide and you notice a row of shanties built on top of the city wall—a place where the poor and the disreputable people live—and that is where your feet now take you. Why? Why do you seek out the house of a prostitute as your "safe house" in the city of Jericho?

3. Now put yourself in Rahab's position. You are looked down upon and exploited by your society. You have heard rumors of an army of invaders camped across

the Jordan River. Suddenly, two men appear on your doorstep, speaking a with a strange accent, seeking refuge from pursuers. You know that if you are caught helping an enemy of your people, you will be tortured and killed. You also have no reason to trust these two spies. Why should you help them? What's in it for you?

4. What does Rahab promise the spies? What do these promises tell us about Rahab's faith?

5. What do the spies promise Rahab? What do these promises tell us about the intentions of Israel?

6. What do you think of Rahab's lie in verses 4 and 5? Was it justified? Could she have protected the spies without lying?

Does the Bible teach "situation ethics" in this story —the idea that lies and other sins can sometimes be condoned to serve a higher purpose? Explain your answer.

Let's Get Personal

7. Describe some arena in your life where you sense that God is calling you to take a lonely, risky stand against a hostile world.

8. What is the "scarlet cord" you are counting on to save you from the judgment that will one day come upon this world?

3

THE RIVER OF IMPOSSIBILITY

JOSHUA 3–4

"The difficult we will do immediately; the impossible may take a little longer!"

That was the slogan of the courageous, hardworking Seabees of World War II (they took their name from the initials C.B., which stood for the Navy's Construction Battalion). They closely followed combat units into newly conquered territories during World War II, building barracks, bridges, roads, and landing strips. They kept their word, performing tasks that were not only difficult but downright impossible—and they did it on-time.

Joshua's army had something even better than the Seabees to handle all the impossible chores: God Himself. Even so, the army of Israel needed the assurance of His presence. After forty years of wandering in the desert, thinking they had finally arrived in their long-awaited homeland, they faced what appeared to be an insurmountable difficulty.

Life is like that. Sometimes when hopes are the highest, problems suddenly appear which are as formidable to us as the swirling waters of the Jordan were to the Israelites.

After delivering a message at a conference, the speaker stayed behind to talk with a number of people who had been in the audience. One was a young mother who had not slept the previous night because her husband had come home at 10:30 p.m. and announced he intended to divorce her. Another was a pastor whose teenage daughter was rebelling against him, against his wife, and against God. Another was a Christian worker whose husband had entered the hospital for treatment of a brain tumor.

Each of these problems is an insurmountable difficulty, an impossibility, an uncrossable river. How do people face and endure such problems? The answer: Many people don't. Some people break under the strain.

It is estimated that over a million Americans now receive inpatient treatment for acute mental and emotional illness in facilities ranging from general hospitals to state-run asylums. Many more Americans seek treatment for anxiety, depression, and phobias through outpatient facilities, such as private psychiatrists' offices and mental health clinics. It is predicted that 15 million Americans will experience a nervous breakdown sometime in their lives.

More than 100,000 people attempt suicide every year and, according to the *1993 Britannica World Data Annual,* nearly 30,000 of those attempts are successful. Suicide is the tenth leading cause of death in the Western world.

According to Drs. Robert Hemfelt, Frank Minirth, and Paul Meier of the Minirth-Meier Clinic, roughly 15 million Americans are addicted to alcohol and/or drugs. The doctors also note that there is a tragic ripple effect to these statistics: those *15 million* addicts and alcoholics go on to scar the lives and the emotions of some *60 million* family members![1] What is the answer to the mind-break-ing, life-destroying impossibilities that create such tragic statistics in our society?

It has been said that the only difference between a live wire and a dead one is the connection. The only hope for healing the pain represented by these statistics is a connection to a supernatural source of strength—strength that can accomplish not only the difficult, but the downright impossible! In this generation as in Joshua's generation, God's people stand at the brink of deep waters, crying out for some way across the rivers of impossibility.

Preparing for the Crossing (3:1–4)

Upon receiving the spies' report of the situation in Jericho, Joshua immediately went into action. He ordered immediate preparations for crossing the Jordan and invading Canaan. He didn't know *how* this vast group of people was going to cross the swollen river, but he believed that God would make it possible. So he moved the entire Israelite nation, bag and baggage, seven miles from Shittim to the brink of the Jordan.

Could such a logistical feat be accomplished by today's church institutions? Not likely! Our bureaucratic structures wouldn't allow it! As Bible commentator John J. Davis pointedly observes,

> When the time came to actually move toward the Jordan, Joshua did not request an extension of time in order to let the Jordan subside. He did not plead for a different route so as to avoid confrontation with the enemy. He did not call for a caucus, a commission, or a committee report in five copies with this committee to be duly organized and named "The Committee on Crisis in the Contemporary Situation."[2]

When the Israelites arrived at the river, they stopped for three days. Why the delay? Time was no doubt needed for the leaders to organize the crossing and pass instructions on to the people. The delay also allowed them an opportunity to get close and see the river, which by that time had become a strong and rapid current, due to the melting of the winter snows on Mount Hermon in the north. At this point, the people might have begun to doubt the wisdom (if not the sanity) of Moses' successor! Looking at the raging waters, they must have wondered, "Does Joshua really expect us to cross *that?*"

At the end of the third day of waiting, Joshua gave the instructions: The pillar of cloud would no longer lead them. Instead, the people were to follow the Ark of the Covenant. The first to advance into the land of promise would be the priests, bearing the Ark. Since the Ark symbolized the presence of the Lord Himself, it was Jehovah who led His people into Canaan. "Behold," announced Joshua in verse 11, "the Ark of the Covenant of the Lord of all the earth is crossing over ahead of you into the Jordan."

With the Ark going ahead, the people would fall in behind or spread around it on three sides. But as verse 4 tells us, they were to keep a distance from the Ark of 2,000 cubits (about 3,000 feet). Why? To remind them of the sacredness of the Ark and the holiness of the God it represented. There was to be no casual or flippant attitude toward God—only a profound spirit of respect and reverence. These days, people carelessly refer to God as "the man upstairs," but the people under Joshua understood that the image of God was not to be so casually cheapened. To them, God was the sovereign and holy Lord of all the earth.

The distance was also essential so that the largest possible number in this great population could observe the Ark as it went before them. God was about to lead them over unfamiliar ground, through enemy-held territory. Without the guidance and leadership of the Lord, the people would not know which direction to take.

Every step you and I take in our lives is like that: a step into unknown, unfamiliar, and perilous territory. We don't know what the next step may bring us: an accident, an illness, a heart attack, the loss of a spouse or a child or a close friend, a major financial reversal, the loss of a job, betrayal, opposition, an unfair accusation—perhaps even death itself. Like the Israelites under Joshua's leadership, you and I need to see and know that God is going before us, leading the way into the promised land. We need to hear the reassuring voice of God saying to us, "Be strong! Be courageous! Follow me!"

Consecrated for the Crossing (3:5–13)

As the day for the crossing approached, Joshua commanded the people to sanctify themselves. Most military leaders would have said, "Sharpen your swords and polish your shields!" But for the people of God, it was spiritual rather than military preparation that Joshua ordered his soldiers to undertake. Why? Because the task at hand did not call for swords or shields, but for a great miracle, the accomplishment of the impossible by the God of Israel. So the Israelites prepared for the manifestation of God's power, just as their fathers had prepared themselves at the foot of Mount Sinai before Jehovah revealed and handed down the Law (see Ex. 19:10).

On the night of his graduation from medical school, Dr. Howard A. Kelly (who later became a world-famous surgeon), wrote in his diary,

> I dedicate myself, my time, my capabilities, my ambition, everything to Him. Blessed Lord, sanctify me

to Thy uses. Give me no worldly success which may not
lead me nearer to my Savior!

If we genuinely seek spiritual victory, we too must be
willing to separate ourselves and purify ourselves from
all defiling sin. We must be willing to be set apart and
dedicated 100 per cent to God's will and purpose for our
lives. This was Israel's challenge on the banks of the Jordan, and it is our challenge today.

But that is not all. The people of Israel were commanded to *expect the impossible*. They were to eagerly
await the miracle God would work on their behalf. Many
Christians today, if they were in the sandals of those Israelites, would survey the swollen waters of the Jordan,
then sink into frustration and despondency. They would
throw up their hands and cry out, "Impossible!" But that
is exactly what God tells us he wants to accomplish in
your life and mine: the utterly, incredibly, unbelievably
impossible! We are to wait in eager anticipation to see
how our God is going to act on our behalf.

In verse 13, the Lord revealed to Joshua the means
by which the nation of Israel would cross that impossible
river, so that Joshua could in turn explain it to the people. The time had come to elevate and magnify Joshua as
the leader of the people. It was time to establish Joshua's
credential's as God's representative to guide Israel into
the land of promise. And what better way to accomplish
this than for Joshua to direct their passage *right through
a miraculously parted river!*

So the people crossed on dry land, with the waters of
the Jordan miraculously heaped up on either side of
them. Joshua 4:14 records that, as a result of that miracle, "the Lord exalted Joshua in the sight of all Israel; so
that they revered him, just as they had revered Moses all
the days of his life."

But when Joshua gave the words of God to the people, he did not say, "This miracle is designed to make me look good!" Rather, he told them that this miracle was to certify that the living God—in contrast to the dead idols worshipped by the Canaanites!—was in their midst. Furthermore, the living God would not only open a way across the flooded Jordan, but would also drive out the seven tribes inhabiting the land.

"The living God is among you!" This became the slogan of conquest, the key to victory over the enemies of the land. God's promise—"I will be with you!"—appears on almost every page of the book of Joshua. It is a promise of His presence that still sustains the Lord's people.

During the Civil War, the town of Moresfield, West Virginia, was on the dividing line between North and South. As a result, the war ebbed, flowed, and eddied about the hapless little town like the tide upon the shore. It would be in Confederate hands one day and Yankee hands the next. In one old house, which stands in Moresfield to this day, an elderly woman lived alone.

One morning, Yankee troops rudely stomped up onto her porch. She was completely at their mercy, and knew that soldiers from either side sometimes searched the homes of citizens, taking food and any other belongings they wanted. Still, she was a genteel lady of the South and prided herself on her Southern manners and hospitality. Calmly and graciously, she invited the soldiers to come in and be seated at her table.

She set breakfast before them, then said, "It is a custom of long standing in this house to have devotions before meals." Then she took up her Bible, opened it at random, and began to read:

The Lord is my Light and my Salvation; whom shall I fear? The Lord is the Strength of my life; of whom shall

I be afraid? When the wicked, even mine enemies and
my foes, came upon me to eat up my flesh, they stumbled and fell. Though an host should encamp against
me, my heart shall not fear; though war should rise
against me, in this will I be confident.[3]

When she had finished reading, she set the Bible
aside and began to pray. As she prayed, she heard the
sound of shuffling shoes on the boards of her floor. When
she said, "Amen," and opened her eyes, the soldiers were
gone! Her calm and courage in the presence of her enemies had made them afraid to stay any longer!

Completion of the Crossing (3:14–17)

The day of the crossing, the day of Israel's entrance
into Canaan, finally arrived. The people folded their
tents and followed the Ark-bearing priests to the brink of
the Jordan. It was the time of the barley harvest, the
month of Nisan (March-April). As they approached the
swollen river, the faith of the priests of Israel was about
to be severely tested. Would they hesitate in fear or would
they advance in faith, believing that what God had promised would come to pass?

The priests of Israel were not expected to act on
blind faith—nor are we. Their faith and ours is based on
the rock-solid reliability of what God has revealed, and
on what He has promised.

Two people were once talking about God's promises.
"What do you do with the promises of God?" asked one.
"I underline them in blue ink," replied the other. Clearly,
God expects us to do more than simply *underline* His
promises! He expects us to *act* on them! Like the priests
on the banks of the Jordan, we must appropriate God's
promises by faith and make them our own. We must put

one foot in front of the other and start moving in the direction of our own river of impossibility!

Dramatic events took place when the priests, carrying the Ark of the Covenant, stepped into swirling waters of the Jordan. As verse 16 (KJV) relates, "The water from upstream stopped flowing. It piled up in a heap a great distance away, at a town called Adam in the vicinity of Zarethan, while the water flowing down to the Sea of Arabah (the Salt Sea) was completely cut off. So the people crossed over opposite Jericho."

While the city named Adam is mentioned only in this one verse in the Old Testament, it is usually identified with Tell ed-Damiyeh, some sixteen miles above the fording place near Jericho. A wide stretch of riverbed was dried up as the waters rose up like walls on either side. The people of Israel gathered up their animals and possessions and hurried across the dry bed of the Jordan and into the Promised Land.

How could such a sensational event occur?

Many insist that this miracle has a natural explanation. They point out that an earthquake on December 8, 1267, caused the high banks of the Jordan to collapse near ed-Damiyeh, damming the river for some ten hours. And on July 11, 1927, another earthquake near the same location caused a blockage of the river for twenty-one hours. Of course, these stoppages did not occur during the flood season. Still, God could have employed a natural cause to achieve his plan, and the timing of that event would still make it a miraculous intervention. But did He? Does the biblical text allow such an interpretation of this event?

Taking all the factors of this event together, it seems best to view this occurrence as a special intervention of God, accomplished in a way that is completely unknown to us. In this account, we see many supernatural events occurring together:

- The event took place exactly as predicted.
- The timing of the event was exact.
- The event took place when the river was at flood stage.
- The wall of water was held in place for what was probably an entire day.
- The soft, muddy river bottom became firm and dry at once.
- The waters returned immediately once the crossing was completed and the priests came up out of the river. It would be appropriate to ask those who insist on a natural explanation if two earthquakes were required in quick succession to part the Jordan for the prophets Elijah and Elisha to cross (2 Kings 2:8,14).

In the crossing of the Jordan River at floodstage by a nation some two million strong, God was glorified, Joshua was elevated in stature and respect, and Israel was emboldened and encouraged for the task ahead. At the same time, this event served to further demoralize and terrorize the Canaanites.

The crossing of the Jordan meant that Israel was irrevocably committed to the struggle against armies, chariots, and fortified cities. Soon the river would close behind them, and there would be no going back. But the people of Israel had no desire to go back. They had made a decision not to walk by the flesh, as they had in the wilderness. They were committed to walking by faith, following the living God as he led them into the land He had promised them.

Today, God calls you and me and all believers to cross a symbolic Jordan river, to move from one level of the Christian life to another. He is calling us to a warfare every bit as real and perilous as that which faced the Israelites as they stepped onto the west bank of the Jordan. He calls us to *spiritual warfare*. When we cross this symbolic Jordan, it means the end of the life we once lived by our own human efforts, and the beginning of life lived by the principles of faith and obedience.

The Jordan was the impassible obstacle which kept Israel from the Promised Land. It was the river of impossibility. We also face obstacles that keep us from enjoying the promised life of faith, obedience, and victory God wants us to experience. Even though these obstacles appear as formidable as the swirling waters of the Jordan, we must never lose sight of the God who is able to take us through. He has promised, "When you pass through the waters, I will be with you; and through the rivers, they will not overflow you" (Isa. 43:2). As in the words of the old chorus,

> Got any rivers you think are uncrossable?
>   Got any mountains you can't tunnel through?
> God specializes in things thought impossible;
>   He'll do what no other friend can do.

Monuments at the Crossing (4:1–24)

It was important that this great miracle never be forgotten. God directed that stone monuments be built so that the Israelites would remember how God acted on their behalf on this historic day.

From the Pyramids of Egypt to the Civil War memorials in Vicksburg, Manassas, and Gettysburg, from the towering Washington Monument to the black-granite, bunker-like Vietnam War Memorial in Washington, D.C., human beings have erected lasting monuments to memorialize people and deeds that should never be forgotten.

But where are the monuments to magnify the greatness and goodness of God?

Joshua 4 describes just such a monument, erected to memorialize and celebrate the crossing of the Israelites over the dry bed of the Jordan into the Promised Land. This monument was to serve as a visible reminder of God's work of deliverance to the people, and to their children, and their children's children. Joshua was told by the Lord to direct twelve specially chosen men to carry twelve stones from the riverbed to the place of the next night's encampment. So he called the tribal representatives together and relayed to them the Lord's command.

The response of the twelve men was immediate and unquestioning. They could well have feared to reenter the Jordan. After all, how long would it remain dry? Whatever fears they may have had were put aside as they unhesitatingly obeyed God's instructions.

In verse 8, we see that Joshua joined the men on their strange mission. While the twelve men were each wrenching up a great stone from the riverbed, Joshua was moved to set another pile of twelve stones to mark the precise spot where the priests stood with the Ark of the Covenant. This act was apparently done on Joshua's own initiative, and was an expression of his desire to have a personal reminder of God's power and faithfulness at the very beginning of the conquest of Canaan.

All that the Lord commanded was now accomplished. In anticipation of the renewed flowing of the Jordan, verses 10 through 18 review the details of the crossing:

• The priests and the Ark remained in the riverbed while the people hurried across.

• The men of the Transjordanian tribes, not hampered with families and goods, led the crossing.

• When all had crossed and the special mission of the

memorials had been completed, the priests left the river-bed and resumed their position at the head of the people.

• The Jordan River resumed its flow.

Imagine the scene as the Israelites stood on the river-bank, watching the Jordan's rushing torrent cover the very path they had just walked. Imagine how they must have felt as the waters filled the riverbed from bank to bank, barring them from the land where they had just been encamped. There was no returning now. A new and exciting chapter in their history had begun.

But this was no time for reflecting. There was still much work to do. Joshua led the people to Gilgal, their first encampment in Canaan, about two miles from Jericho. There the stones from the Jordan riverbed were set up, perhaps in a circular formation. The name *Gilgal* means "circle."

How were future generations to know the significance of the stones? The answer is found in verses 21 through 23, where Joshua says to the people,

> When your children ask their fathers in time to come, saying, "What are these stones?" Then you shall inform your children, saying, "Israel crossed this Jordan on dry ground." For the Lord your God dried up the waters of the Jordan before you until you had crossed, just as the Lord your God had done to the Red Sea.

Notice the solemn responsibility that Joshua entrusts to the parents of Israel: "You shall inform your children." Parents are to be teachers of God's ways and works to their children. As God commanded the Israelites in the wilderness, "And these words, which I am commanding you today, shall be on your heart; and you shall teach them diligently to your sons and shall talk of them when you sit in your house and when you walk by the way and when you lie down and when you rise up."[4] As the great nineteenth century preacher Alexander Maclaren said so well,

> The Jewish father was not to send his child to some Levite or other to get his question answered, but was to answer it himself. I am afraid that a good many English parents, who call themselves Christians, are too apt to say, "Ask your Sunday school teacher," when such questions are put to them. The decay of parental religious teaching is working enormous mischief in Christian households; and the happiest results would follow if Joshua's homely advice were attended to, "Ye shall let your children know."[5]

Maclaren's challenge to Christian parents to reverse the "decay of parental religious teaching" is far more timely and urgent today than in his own time! Christians dishonor God and endanger their own children when they abdicate their God-given responsibility to teach their children the truth about God's love, faithfulness, and power.

Satan is doing all he can to seduce our children and convince them that God is not relevant to modern life. He is using peer pressure, the entertainment media, the news media, material things, drugs, sexual enticement, and even the government and the educational system to eradicate a love and respect for God from their hearts. If Christian parents do not counter these powerful influences with biblical teaching—not just once a week, but daily, during those "teachable moments" that take place throughout every day—then those parents stand a good chance of *losing* their children.

An Anchor for Our Faith

The memorial stones served yet another purpose, "that all the peoples of the earth may know that the hand of the Lord is mighty." Thus, as the families of Israel spent their first night in the land, their hearts may well have been filled with uncertainty and fear. The mountains rising steeply to the west looked dark and forbidding. But as the people looked at the twelve stones which had once been covered by the flowing waters of the Jordan, they were reminded that God had done something great for them that day. Surely they could trust Him for the "impossible" challenges of the days ahead.

The Lord often works in just this way, giving us experiences in the early days of our Christian lives that we can later remember as evidences of God's power. Then, when the storms of life break over us, we can look back and be reminded of how God worked. These memories of God's power, which he demonstrated for us in the past, serve to anchor our faith during the trials of the future. Such reminders can be a great testimony of God's power and faithfulness to our families and to the world.

"Memorial stones" are just as important today as in Joshua's time, and they serve the same purpose: to encourage our present faith by reminding us of God's past and continuing faithfulness and power. One such "memorial stone" is a part of the history of Dallas Seminary.

In the spring of 1924, plans were being laid for the new seminary, the purpose of which was to emphasize the teaching of the Bible above all else. The seminary's president-elect, Dr. Lewis Sperry Chafer, had gone to Dundee, Scotland, to hold evangelistic meetings at the invitation of a leading manufacturer in that city. While in Dundee, Dr. Chafer stayed as a guest in the home of the wealthy Scottish industrialist.

One morning during his stay, Dr. Chafer awoke with a deep sense of anxiety about the future of the seminary, which at that time consisted of nothing more than plans on a drawing board. For some unexplainable reason, he felt an overwhelming sense that the entire plan was doomed to fail. So he went to his knees and prayed, "God, show me your will! What do you want me to do?" His sense of foreboding was so strong that if God did not give him an answer, he planned to send a telegram back to Dallas and request that the plans for the seminary be completely abandoned.

Later, at breakfast, Dr. Chafer was seated next to his wealthy Scottish host and was surprised when the man asked, "Dr. Chafer, has any provision been made for the library at the new seminary?"

"No," Chafer replied, "but we were hoping to obtain the valuable library of the late Dr. Griffith Thomas."

"Fine!" his host exclaimed. "Please go ahead and purchase the books and send the bill to me. And by the way, what about your salary as president of the Seminary?"

"I had not expected to draw any salary," Chafer replied.

"You will need some financial help," the manufacturer replied. "I wish to personally send you two thousand dollars a year." It was a quite adequate salary for those days.

As Dr. Chafer later recalled, "Truly, my cup ran over! The gift of a library valued at four thousand dollars, and such unexpected provision for my salary—all in one day!" He had received his answer from the Lord, and plans for the Seminary went forward. Today, Dallas Seminary is one of the leading training grounds for pastors who seek to "rightly divide the Word of truth." Equally important, the Seminary stands as a monument—like the circle of stones at Gilgal—to the faithfulness of God.

In Joshua 3 and 4, we have encountered another profound "secret" of godly leadership in the example of Joshua: *A true Christian leader trusts and obeys God, expecting Him to do the impossible. By faith, a true Christian leader steps out into the river of impossibility, knowing that nothing is impossible with God.* Today, let us be reminded of the great things God has done in our lives. Let us anchor our faith and renew our trust as we move out toward our own rivers of impossibility, with our eyes fixed firmly and confidently on the other shore.

The land of promise awaits!

QUESTIONS FOR REFLECTION AND DISCUSSION

See Your Own Reflection

1. What "memorial stones" of God's past faithfulness can you point to in your own life?

Dig a Little Deeper

2. In 3:5, Joshua tells the people, "Consecrate yourselves, for tomorrow the Lord will do wonders among you." What does that word "consecrate" mean? What specific actions was Joshua calling the people to perform?

How can we consecrate ourselves today, so that we can be prepared for the wonders God wants to do in our lives?

3. Put yourself in the position of the people of Israel. Imagine and describe what you would feel as you:

• Stand on the east bank of the Jordan, surveying the impossible task of crossing with all your family, animals, and possessions to the other side.

• Walk across the dry riverbed, seeing the Ark of the Covenant before you and the high walls of water on either side of you.

• Stand on the west bank of the Jordan—the "welcome mat" of the Promised Land—watching the walls of water come back together, covering your footsteps and closing off all possibility of retreat.

4. Compare this miracle which God did at the beginning of Joshua's tenure as leader of Israel with the miracle God did for Moses when He parted the Red Sea (see Exodus 14). Why do you think God chose such similar kinds of miracles to perform at similar points in the career of each leader?

5. Why do you think God chose this particular time—a time when the Jordan river was swollen and flooded—to take the people of Israel across and into the Promised Land?

Let's Get Personal

6. What is your "river of impossibility" right now?

7. Where do you stand right now with regard to your "river of impossibility"? Are you on the east bank, wondering how you can ever get across? Are you in the middle of the riverbed, walking on dry land? Are you up to your neck in water, wondering when the waters will part? Or are you on the west bank, giving thanks to God for his miraculous work in your life?

4

CONSECRATION BEFORE CONQUEST

JOSHUA 5

Some remember it as a techno-war of Scud-busting Patriot missiles, Tomahawk cruise missiles, radar-baffling Stealth fighters, and laser-guided "smart bombs." But the 1991 Persian Gulf War was also an on-the-ground logistical challenge which combined ground troops from thirty-nine nations into a single fighting force of *one million* uniformed men and women. A historically unique combination of patient strategy, technological wizardry, and courageous people resulted in a ground war that was won in exactly 100 hours—an achievement for which Gen. H. Norman Schwarzkopf receives much of the credit.

The victory in the Gulf was a triumph made up of many factors, not the least of which was the mobilization of the one-million-person fighting force. But in Joshua 5, we see that Joshua faced a logistical challenge that was roughly twice as big as that which faced "Stormin' Norman" Schwarzkopf: Joshua had to move some *two million* soldiers and civilians into position to attack the strongholds of Canaan—and Joshua had to do it all without the luxury of radio communication and troop transport planes and vehicles.

After the miraculous crossing of the Jordan, Joshua's forces quickly established a beachhead at Gilgal. From every human perspective, the time had come to strike. The Canaanite enemy was completely demoralized, while the morale of the Israelites was at an all-time high. The news was spreading throughout the land that the dreaded Israelites had come into the land, and that they were supernaturally aided by their seemingly all-powerful deity! Some of the "newspaper headlines" that had the Canaanites in such a panic:

• "The God of Israel dries up the Red Sea!"

• "Amorite kings Sihon and Og defeated by the Hebrews!"

• "Waters of the Jordan River parted! Israelite army on the march!"

A mood of fear and crisis had fallen upon the land of Canaan. What better time than *this* to strike a decisive blow?

But this was not God's plan. He is never in a hurry, even though His children all too often are. There is a lot of wisdom in the old carpenter's dictum, "Measure twice, cut once." In other words, "Slow down. Take care. Study the situation. Plan. Pray."

Here we see another of Joshua's "leadership secrets" in action: *A leader does not allow himself to be pressured or rushed into hasty action.* If you feel pressured to make a decision or to take action prematurely, *stop!* Resist that pressure. Consult with the Lord. Seek wise counsel from other Christians. God does not require you to make major decisions without adequate opportunity for prayer and consideration.

The Meaning of Consecration

From God's point of view, Israel was not yet ready to fight on the soil of Canaan. There was unfinished business to be taken care of—business of a spiritual nature. It was not yet time for conquest. It was time for consecration.

What does "consecration" mean? It means the complete dedication of a person or an object to a specific purpose or use. A vivid example of consecration can be found in the closing lines of the Declaration of Independence which established the existence of the United States (July 4, 1776): "And for the support of this Declaration, with a firm reliance on the protection of divine Providence, we mutually pledge to each other our Lives, our Fortunes, and our sacred Honor." The founding fathers consecrated everything they were and everything they had to the purpose of establishing the United States as a free and independent nation.

In a similar way, God commanded the people of Israel to consecrate and dedicate themselves—body, mind, and spirit—to carrying out God's plan for Israel. They were to be physically, mentally, emotionally, and spiritually committed to the mission of liberating Canaan from heathen domination, and of making the land a fit dwelling place for God's people. The Israelites were to make sure that they held nothing back, that they placed their lives on the line for the sake of God's eternal purpose.

During World War II, as the bombs of Nazi Germany were raining down on English cities, one Englishman wrote a letter in which he described the English spirit of dedication and consecration with these words:

> As one man, the whole nation has handed over all its resources to the Government. We have invested the Cabinet with the right to conscript any of us for any task, to take our goods, our money, our all. Never have rich men set such little store by their wealth; never have we been so ready to lay down life itself, if only our cause may triumph.

That is the kind of consecration God now called His people to undertake. This, in fact, is another "leadership secret" we can draw from the leadership model of Joshua: *Consecration precedes conquest. Whatever task you undertake, prepare yourself mentally, physically, emotionally, and spiritually for that task. Then pour everything you have into that task, and carry it out with complete singleness of mind.* This is a principle not only of good spiritual leadership and good military leadership, but of sound business leadership as well.

Management expert Peter Drucker expresses the principle of consecration and dedication this way: "Whenever anything is being accomplished, it is being done, I have learned, by a monomaniac with a mission." In business, in spiritual warfare, or on the field of battle, consecration *must* precede conquest.

The famed Confederate general, Thomas J. "Stonewall" Jackson, was a devout Christian. After the failure of one of his military operations during the Civil War, he concluded that the reason for the failure was that the raid was carried out on a Sunday. Jackson vowed never again to dishonor the Christian Sabbath by launching a military operation on Sunday.

So Gen. Jackson planned his next raid for Monday and ordered that the gunpowder for the operation be on hand by Saturday, so that it would not have to be transported on the Lord's Day. The quartermaster, however, was unable to obtain the powder in time, so he had it shipped on Sunday. When Jackson found out, he refused to accept the gunpowder. Instead, he ordered the quartermaster to return the "Sabbath-breaking" powder, and he put off the raid until a suitable shipment of "consecrated gunpowder" arrived. When the new powder arrived, the raid was successfully carried out.

"Stonewall" Jackson believed that consecration must precede conquest. So did Joshua. And so should we. But what does consecration consist of? For Joshua and his forces, consecration consisted of four specific ingredients:

- the renewal of circumcision;
- the celebration of the Passover;
- the appropriation of Canaan's produce; and
- the acknowledgement of their divine Commander-in-Chief.

The Renewal of Circumcision (5:2–9)

The panic-stricken Canaanites would have been doubly perplexed if they could have seen what Joshua did next: He *circumcised* the sons of Israel. Had the Canaanites known, they would have wondered, "What outrageous insanity has gotten into these Israelites? How is this painful operation supposed to prepare them for war? On the eve of battle, the Israeli commander is actually going through his ranks and systematically *incapacitating* his troops!" Yet when Joshua received this command from the Lord, he instantly obeyed—even though, as a military commander, it must have been difficult for him to do so.

The men of Israel who had been circumcised in Egypt had all died in the wilderness, because of their disobedience at Kadesh-barnea. The sons born during the wilderness wanderings were not circumcised; and it was this new generation upon whom the sacred rite would be performed.

Since the Israelites were slaves in Egypt, they did not practice circumcision until they were about to leave. The Egyptians performed circumcision and would probably have prohibited the practice to the Israelites, since it was reserved for Egyptian priests and upper-class citizens. The Lord acknowledged the completed circumcisions with the declaration, "Today I have rolled away the reproach of Egypt from you."

Further indication of the importance of this event is the fact that a new significance was attached to the name *Gilgal.* Not only was the meaning "circle" to remind Israel of the memorial stones, but now the related idea of "rolling away" would commemorate Israel's act of obedience at the same site.

Why was circumcision so important? Stephen, in his dynamic speech before the Sanhedrin, declared that God gave to Abraham "the covenant of circumcision" (Acts 7:8). Circumcision was no ordinary religious rite, but was rooted in the Abrahamic covenant, a contract guaranteeing the everlasting continuation of Abraham's seed and their everlasting right to possess the land. In this connection God designated circumcision as the sign or symbol of that contract, and instructed Abraham that every male person of his household as well as every male child yet to be born was to be circumcised (Gen. 17:7–8,23–27).

The act of circumcision itself spoke of separation from the widely prevalent sins of the time. Furthermore, the rite had spiritual overtones, not only in relation to sexual conduct, but in every phase of life. "Circumcise then your heart, and stiffen your neck no more" (Deut. 10:16; see also Deut. 30:6 and Jer. 4:4).

The Israelites of Joshua's time needed to know that circumcision was not simply a mark in the flesh. There was to be holiness in their lives as well. That is why in Gilgal, God tells the Israelites, in effect, "Before I fight your battles in Canaan, you must have this mark of the covenant in your flesh." Joshua understood the importance of this divine requirement and led the people in unhesitating obedience.

To us as Christians at the end of the twentieth century, the rite of circumcision is not merely some historical tradition of the ancient Hebrews. This rite has special symbolic meaning to us today. As the apostle Paul tells us in Colossians 2:11, we as Christians have been "circumcised" in Christ: "In Him you were also circumcised with a circumcision made without hands, in the removal of the body of the flesh by the circumcision of Christ."

The "circumcision" Paul describes is spiritual and relates to our inward beings. This spiritual "circumcision" takes place at the time of salvation when the Holy Spirit joins the believer to Christ. At that time, the "body of the flesh," our carnal nature, is judged. This doesn't mean that Christians do not sin, because our old carnal nature remains a part of us throughout this life (see Romans 7). But as Christians we recognize the reality that, because of our inward, spiritual "circumcision," we are to commit ourselves to serving God rather than serving sin. We are to treat our carnal nature as a judged, condemned prisoner who deserves no favors or rights over our lives.

There is a story that comes out of World War II that illustrates what our spiritual "circumcision" should mean in our lives. In 1942, the Japanese captured the Bataan Peninsula in the Philippines, forcing the American and Filipino forces to retreat into the island fortress of Corregidor in Manila harbor. On May 6, the American commander, Gen. Jonathan Mayhew Wainwright, surrendered his starving, demoralized troops. The general and his men were taken to a concentration camp in Japanese-held China, where they were given the most inhumane treatment imaginable. They were starved, beaten, and subjected to daily intimidation and humiliation. Gen. Wainwright, because of his superior rank, was often singled out for an extra measure of humiliation.

In August 1945, Japan surrendered. American forces moved into China to liberate the prison camps. When the Americans entered Gen. Wainwright's camp, they immediately sought him out and gave him the news of the American victory—then they placed him in charge of the camp. Though thin and scarred by over three years in captivity, his eyes were clear and his voice was strong and commanding as he went out into the prison yard where the Japanese guards—his former tormentors—were assembled, their eyes filled with fear. The Japanese wondered what would happen to them now that the tables were turned.

"I am in command here," Wainwright roared, "and these are my orders!"

Once you and I were prisoners to our carnal nature and to sin. But when we became "circumcised" in Christ, the carnal nature is no longer our master. The tables have been turned. Though our carnal nature once tortured and harassed us, we are now to treat it as our prisoner. Our message to the old carnal nature is now, "By the power of the Holy Spirit, I am in command here, and these are my orders!" Our spiritual nature must now be in command over the carnal nature. That is what it means to have a circumcised heart.

The Celebration of the Passover (5:10)

Camped at Gilgal, Israel next observed the Passover. Without circumcision, the Israelites would have been disqualified from the feast (Ex. 12:44,48).

This is only the third celebration of the Passover recorded in the Bible. The first was observed in Egypt in anticipation of Israel's deliverance from bondage and oppression (Ex. 12:1–20). The second was observed at

Sinai, just before the people broke camp and moved toward Canaan (Num. 9:5). There is no indication that the Passover was ever observed during the wanderings in the wilderness.

But here, at Gilgal in Canaan, there was a memorable and significant celebration of the feast. It must have been a tremendously meaningful and emotional celebration for these people who had just passed between the waters of the Jordan, and who had just experienced a miracle every bit as amazing as the events which the Passover commemorated. The just-completed crossing of the Jordan was a clear, loud echo of the Red Sea crossing of Moses' day. This event must have stirred vivid memories in the minds of those who were under twenty years of age at the time of the Exodus from Egypt—in other words, those who were still alive and had not been excluded from crossing into Canaan.

The Passover commemorated an event which occurred some forty years earlier, and which was burned into the memories of the oldest living Israelites: on that day, every Hebrew family killed a lamb and sprinkled the blood on the doorposts and lintels of their homes. In their memories, some of these Israelites could no doubt still hear the awful death cries of the Egyptians' firstborn, killed by the Angel of Death, followed by the sorrowful wailing of the Egyptian families. They surely recalled the urgency and the excitement of the midnight departure, the terror of being pursued by the Egyptian army, the awe of passing over the exposed bottom of the Red Sea as the walls of water piled up on either side, and the moment of triumph when they looked back and saw the sea close in and bury the Egyptian soldiers, horses, and chariots.

As the lambs were slain in Gilgal for this first Passover in the land of promise, the Israelites were assured that God was still faithful and able to deliver. Just as the crossing of the Red Sea was followed by the destruction of the Egyptian slave-masters, so would the crossing of the Jordan be followed by the defeat of the Canaanite enemy.

But the Passover did not only point backward forty years to the deliverance from Egypt. It also pointed forward some 1400 years to the death of Jesus Christ, the Lamb of God. As the apostle Paul wrote in 1 Corinthians 5:7, "Christ, our Passover, also has been sacrificed." As Christians, we remember that sacrifice by partaking of the Lord's Supper. And just as the ancient Israelites looked forward to the sacrifice of Christ whenever they celebrated the Passover, we also look forward when we celebrate the Lord's Supper, for we celebrate His death in this manner only until He comes again. The Lord's Supper, then, is a connecting link between the past and the future, between the First and Second Advents of Jesus Christ, our Passover.

During a visit to Jerusalem, Dr. Hudson Armerding checked into a hotel and was assisted with his suitcases by a Palestinian Arab. Not knowing whether he was expected to pay the man on the spot or if the service would be added to his hotel bill, Dr. Armerding said to the man, "I'm very sorry. I've just arrived in the country and I do not have the change to give you."

The man replied, "Sir, I don't need money. I need hope."

Our hope is in Jesus Christ, whose sacrificial death and resurrection has delivered us from the bondage of sin. The deliverance of the past sustains us in the present, and provides bright hope for tomorrow.

The Appropriation of Canaan's Produce (5:11–12)

On the day after the Passover, the Israelites ate some of the produce of the land—unleavened cakes and dried corn. Since they gave evidence of wanting to be fully obedient to the Law of God, it is probable that they first brought the wave offering of a sheaf of grain as prescribed in Leviticus 23:10–14. Then the people ate freely of the harvest. Roasted ears of grain are still considered a delicacy in the Middle East, and are eaten as a substitute for bread.

From the time of Moses, God had promised to bring Israel into a land of abundance, "a land of wheat and barley, of vines and fig trees and pomegranates, a land of olive oil and honey; a land where you shall eat food without scarcity" (Deut. 8:8–9). Now, at last, they had tasted the fruit of the land and they realized it was only a foretaste of blessings to come.

The next day the manna ceased. For forty long years the people had eaten manna from heaven. But when the people had their first feast provided by the fertile soil of the Promised Land, the manna stopped appearing as suddenly as it had begun. Here was a clear demonstration to the people that the provision of food was not a matter of chance, but of special providence from God.

It is noteworthy that God had not discontinued the manna earlier, when Israel despised it (Num. 11:6). He didn't even discontinue the manna when the unbelieving generation turned away from Kadesh-barnea and began wandering in the trackless wilderness. He continued to give it for the sake of their children, who would one day grow up and enter the Promised Land under Joshua's leadership.

Can we expect God to work a miracle when natural means are available? There is no evidence that God works unnecessary miracles. We don't need food from heaven when we have bread from the earth.

Acknowledgement of the Divine Commander (5:13–15)

God had just brought the Israelites through three important observances of consecration: the rite of circumcision, the celebration of the Passover, and the eating of the produce of the land of Canaan. Now something happened which was for Joshua alone. It too was extremely meaningful, and its meaning would soon be shared with all the people.

It seemed obvious that the next step would be the capture of Jericho. But since no further message of instruction had come to Joshua, he went out to reconnoiter the seemingly impregnable fortress.

Joshua may have felt perplexed as he viewed the secure walls of Jericho. The spies reported at Kadesh-barnea that the cities of Canaan were "large and fortified to heaven" (Deut. 1:28). Despite Joshua's long military experience, he had never led an attack on a well-fortified city. Of the many fortresses in Palestine, Jericho was the most nearly invincible.

There was also the question of armaments. Israel's army had no siege engines, battering rams, catapults, or moving towers. Their only weapons were swords, slings, arrows, and spears—and these would be like straws against the fortified walls of Jericho.

But one thing was clear: Israel had no choice but to win the battle of Jericho. Now that the River Jordan again flowed at their backs, there was no way open for retreat. Furthermore, they could not bypass the city, because that would leave the camp at Gilgal—which was filled with women, children, goods, and cattle—exposed to attack. The way into the Promised Land led through Jericho. The great walled city had to be faced and overcome.

As he was alone, pondering these heavy thoughts, Joshua was startled to look up and see a soldier standing nearby with his sword drawn. In that moment of surprise, Joshua had no way of knowing whether the man offered his sword in service and aid to Joshua—or whether he brandished it as a threat. Instinctively, Joshua challenged the stranger, saying, in effect: "Who goes there, friend or foe?" If the man were a friend, an Israelite, he was off-limits and had some serious explaining to do—especially since Joshua had given no command for anyone to draw a sword! And if the stranger were an enemy, Joshua was ready to fight!

"Are you for us, or for our adversaries?" asked Joshua.

"No," the man replied, "rather I indeed come now as Captain of the host of the Lord."

Something happened in this exchange to convince Joshua that this was no mortal soldier. As with Abraham under the oak at Mamre, Jacob at Peniel, and Moses at the burning bush, there came a flash of revelation so clear and intense that Joshua *knew* he was in the presence of God. It seems clear that Joshua was indeed talking to the Angel or Messenger of Jehovah, in what theologians call a "theophany," a pre-incarnate appearance of the Lord Jesus Christ in human form.

Here was the Captain of the Lord's host, standing with sword drawn, indicating that He would fight with and for Israel. The sword also indicated that God's patient delay of judgment was at an end. The sin of the Canaanites would no longer be tolerated, and the Israelites were to be the instruments of God's judicial punishment.

What kind of military force did this divine Commander lead? The "host of the Lord" surely was not limited to the army of Israel. The Visitor with the sword probably referred to *the host of heaven*, the legions of angels whose work we have witnessed elsewhere in Scripture. For example, the host of heaven surrounded and protected the city of Dothan when Elisha and his servant appeared to be greatly outnumbered by the Syrian army. (See 2 Kings 6:8–17.) In the Garden of Gethsemane at the time of His arrest, Jesus spoke of the twelve legions of angels standing ready to defend Him. (See Matt. 26:53.) In Hebrews 1:14, angels are described as "ministering spirits, sent out to render service for the sake of those who will inherit salvation." Though invisible, they serve and care for us in times of great need.

Only eternity will reveal the full extent of the service and protection rendered to humanity by "the host of heaven." But sometimes the ministry of angels among us can be very clearly seen.

One such time was in June 1920, in the village of Shansi, China. The people of the village were warned that bandits were coming, so the villagers quickly made what preparations they could.

There was a missionary school in the village which was run by one lone lady missionary. This woman was responsible for the forty girls who attended the school—but how could she protect them from these lawless men? There were not enough soldiers in the village to offer effective resistance. The school and everyone in it were completely defenseless.

The woman called all the girls together in one classroom and explained the danger. Then, calmly, she told the girls to get down on their knees and commit themselves into the care of their almighty God. "O God, our heavenly Father," she prayed, "we have no might but in You. Please send your guardian angels to protect us tonight."

As night fell, the missionary and her students heard the sound of screams, shouts, and gunshots. They heard the splintering of wood as doors were kicked in. They heard the cries for mercy as helpless men and women were dragged into the streets. They heard the crackling of fires. The sounds started far in the distance, but they grew closer and closer. Soon the sounds of terror and death were all around them. The girls huddled close to their teacher, expecting the doors of the school to be kicked in at any moment.

Toward morning, the sounds dwindled into the distance. The bandits had overrun the village, taken what they wanted, and departed for the hills. But not one of them had attempted to enter the mission school compound.

When the missionary lady went outside to offer help to the villagers, she found a scene of horror and carnage. Homes and shops were gutted and smoldering. Dead bodies littered the streets. Children clung to weeping mothers. Some of the young women of the town were gone, having been carried away by the bandits. Of all the buildings in the village, only one had been spared: the mission school.

"Why?" the missionary wondered aloud. "Why were we alone spared?"

"The bandits didn't dare harm you," replied one of the villagers, looking at the missionary with awe. "On the corners of your compound walls, we saw four angels with drawn swords, standing guard!"

It is the Commander of this angel host who stood before Joshua, also with a drawn sword. Recognizing the true nature of his heavenly Visitor, Joshua fell on his face and worshipped, saying, "What has my Lord to say to His servant?"

The reply of the Lord to Joshua was brief but urgent, an echo of the command to Moses when he stood before the burning bush: "Remove your sandals from your feet, for the place where you are standing is holy."

This was a deeply significant experience for Joshua. He expected the battle between the Israelite and Canaanite forces to be *his* war—but then he came face-to-face with his Commander-in-Chief, and he learned that the battle was the Lord's. The Captain of the Lord's host had not come as a spectator to the conflict, or even as an ally, offering mere assistance. He had come to show that He was in complete charge, and would shortly reveal His plans for the capture of the citadel of Jericho.

How encouraging and comforting this truth must have been for Joshua. He did not have to bear the heavy burden of leadership on his own shoulders. The conquest of Canaan was *God's* conflict, and he was God's servant. Joshua's part was not to win the war, but to simply make himself and his people available to the true Commander-in-Chief.

During World War I, when Gen. Pershing placed the American army under the command of the brilliant French commander, Marshal Ferdinand Foch, he said, "Marshal Foch, all that we have is yours—infantry, artillery, aviation, everything. Dispose of them as you will." Gen. Pershing's statement is an echo of Joshua's statement to his sword-bearing Visitor when he said, in effect, "All that we have is Yours. Use us as You will."

That is an attitude of complete consecration and obedience. It is an attitude that many of us in leadership roles in business, in government, in the military, and in the church need to learn. Many of us needlessly suffer the emotional, spiritual, and even physical symptoms of stress and frustration because we operate as if the battle is ours, not God's. We pray, "Lord, help me win this battle!" when we should actually pray, "Lord, I am yours to command! Lead me!"

That was the situation Dr. C. I. Scofield found himself in as pastor of the First Congregational Church in Dallas. There was a period in his ministry when all the burdens of shepherding that large congregation seemed heavier than he could bear. He was frustrated, depressed, and approaching a state that today is called "burn-out." The problems that confronted him seemed impossible.

Finally, feeling completely hopeless and defeated, Scofield shut the door of his office and went to his knees. He placed his Bible on the floor before him and began flipping its pages, searching for some answer or message of hope. Led by the Holy Spirit, he paused in the book of Joshua, the closing verses of chapter 5. He read the dialogue between Joshua and his sword-wielding Visitor— and suddenly Scofield understood the source of his pain and frustration: He had been trying to fight the battle alone!

That day, Dr. Scofield turned his ministry over to the Lord, fully realizing for the first time in his life that the work of shepherding First Congregational Church was *God's* work. By accepting God's leadership as Commander-in-Chief, Dr. Scofield allied himself with the Captain of the host of heaven and was able to receive God's victorious power.

This, then, is the final—and most crucial—"leadership secret" to be found in Joshua 5: *Whatever your leadership role, acknowledge God as your Commander-*

in-Chief. The battle is His, not yours. He will fight your battles for you—if you allow Him to do so.

Have you met the Captain of the host of heaven? This same warrior who, sword in hand, met with Joshua on the eve of battle is with you now. He is the unseen but absolutely real Presence who stands ready to fight your battles, in every arena of your life. He is the Lord Jesus Christ, and He will go before you, sword in hand, toppling the walls of the enemy citadels that stand in your way—

If you let Him. *If* you acknowledge Him as your Lord and Commander. *If* you consecrate yourself and put everything you are and have at His disposal.

The battle is the Lord's—but the choice is yours.

QUESTIONS FOR REFLECTION AND DISCUSSION

See Your Own Reflection

1. Describe a time when you were fully consecrated for an important task, either in your family, in your job, in your military career, or in your Christian ministry. What was the outcome of that task? What would the outcome have been had you *not* been fully consecrated?

Dig a Little Deeper

2. In this passage, we see that Joshua consecrates his people for the coming battle through four specific actions:
- the renewal of circumcision;
- the celebration of the Passover;

• the appropriation of Canaan's produce; and

• the acknowledgement of their divine Commander-in-Chief.

Name four specific actions you can take in your own leadership role by which you can consecrate yourself for the tasks and battles that confront you.

3. What does the Lord mean when He says to Joshua, "Today I have rolled away the reproach of Egypt from you"? What is "the reproach of Egypt"—and what rolled it away?

4. In verse 12, we see that God stopped sending manna the day after the Israelites feasted on the food of the Promised Land. What do you think God's purpose was in stopping the manna?

Can you think of a time when God sustained you on "manna" in some way? What happened in your life when the manna stopped?

5. The Passover pointed back in time, to the deliverance of the Israelites from bondage. In what ways did the observance of the Passover prepare the people of Israel for the battle ahead?

No Time For Neutrality

Can you remember a time of deliverance in your own life? How does the memory of that event in your life prepare you for the battles you have to face today?

Let's Get Personal

6. As you honestly search your own heart, who is the Commander-in-Chief in this battle—you or the Lord? Are you experiencing feelings of frustration, depression, self-pity, hopelessness, or bitterness as you fight this battle? Do you feel the weight of command is heavy on your shoulders?

If you cannot honestly say, "This battle is the Lord's," then what do you need to do to turn control over to Him?

5

GOD'S STRATEGY FOR VICTORY

JOSHUA 6

In 1683, the king of Poland, John III Sobieski, led the defense of the city of Vienna and defeated the Turkish invaders. A student of history, King John remembered the victorious boast of Julius Caesar after defeating the king of Pontus in 47 B.C.: "I came, I saw, I conquered." In the wake of that victory, Caesar took all the credit: "I . . . I . . . I . . . ." But King John, like Joshua, was a humble and godly leader, so when he reported his victory to the pope, his words paraphrased those of Caesar's—with a very important difference. He said, "I came, I saw—*God* conquered!"

In Joshua 6, we come to what is surely the most famous military siege in the Bible—a siege that is memorialized in the words of the old spiritual:

> Joshua fit de battle of Jericho,
> Jericho, Jericho,
> Joshua fit de battle of Jericho,
> And de walls come a-tumblin' down!

But Joshua didn't fight that battle. He clearly understood what you and I too easily forget: It is not we who fight the battle at all, but God Himself. We come, we see, but it is God who conquers!

At Jericho, there is absolutely no room for any other interpretation of events: the military strategy was divinely provided. Furthermore, God was always present to give direction and shape events.

The pattern of God's strategy for the conquest of Jericho was based on important geographic factors. From their camp in Gilgal near the Jordan River, the Israelites could see steep hills to the west. Jericho controlled the way of ascent into those mountains. Ai, another heavily defended fortress, stood at the head of the ascent. If the Israelites were to capture the hill country, they would have to defeat Jericho and Ai. Once that was accomplished, the Israelite army would command the top of the hill country and would control the Central Ridge, having driven a wedge between the northern and southern sections of Canaan. Israel could then engage in battle the armies of the south without interference from the more remote enemy in the north.

But before all of this took place, Jericho would have to be defeated. And the defeat of Jericho depended on Joshua and his people following the Lord's plan of action.

The Strategy for the Conquest of Jericho (6:1–7)

In the opening verses of chapter 6, the conversation between Joshua and the Captain of the host of the Lord continued. In the distance, in full view of Commander Joshua, stood the impressive fortress of Jericho.

"I have given Jericho into your hand, with its kings and valiant warriors," said the Captain of the host of

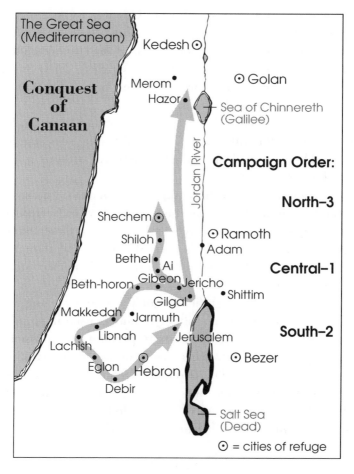

The Great Sea (Mediterranean)

Kedesh ⊙

Conquest of Canaan

Merom •
Hazor •

⊙ Golan

Sea of Chinnereth (Galilee)

Jordan River

Campaign Order:

North–3

Shechem ⊙
Shiloh •
Bethel • Ai •
Beth-horon • Gibeon Jericho
Makkedah • Jarmuth
Libnah •
Lachish •
Eglon • Hebron
Debir •

Gilgal

⊙ Ramoth
• Adam

Central–1

• Shittim

• Jerusalem

South–2

⊙ Bezer

Salt Sea (Dead)

⊙ = cities of refuge

heaven. The tense of the Hebrew verb used when He said, *"I have given,"* is the prophetic perfect tense—a tense which describes a future action as if it were already accomplished. Because God declared it, victory was assured. The fall of Jericho was a "done deal."

The battle plan Joshua was to put into action was completely unique in the history of warfare. Ordinary weapons of war—battering rams, scaling ladders, catapults—were not to be employed. This was to be a war of shoe-leather and musical instruments! God instructed Joshua and his army to march around the city once a day for six successive days while seven priests blew seven trumpets. These priests would march before the Ark of the Covenant, which would also be carried around the city. On the seventh day, after the city had been circled seven times, the walls of Jericho would collapse—*just like that!* The city would be taken, in effect, "without a shot being fired"!

Seven priests, seven trumpets, seven days, and seven circuits around the city on the seventh day: In Scripture, the number *seven* usually symbolizes completeness or perfection. This was God's plan of action; and though it may have seemed foolish to men, it was the perfect strategy for this battle.

What was the significance of the blaring trumpets? These instruments were jubilee trumpets used in connection with Israel's solemn feasts to proclaim the presence of God. This was not, therefore, a military undertaking, but a religious one. The trumpets declared that the Lord of heaven and earth was weaving His invisible way around this doomed city. In the long blasts of these priestly trumpets, God Himself was saying,

> Lift up your heads, O ye gates;
> even lift them up, ye everlasting doors;
> and the King of glory shall come in.[1]

From the point of view of Jericho's defenders, no battle strategy could have been more bizarre and nonsensical than this one. What was all this marching and trumpeting supposed to accomplish? What was to prevent the army of Jericho from raining spears and arrows onto the defenseless Israelites? What would stop the Canaanites from rushing out of the city gates to charge into Israel's marching column and simply butcher them?

Joshua was an experienced military leader, a veteran of many battles. Certainly these and similar objections flashed through his mind as the divine strategy of God was explained to him. But unlike Moses, who spent a lot of time arguing with God over His plans for the Hebrew people, Joshua responded with unquestioning obedience. He lost no time calling together the priests and leaders of the people, passing on to them the directions he had received from his Commander-in-Chief.

Alvin York was a backwoodsman from the Cumberland Mountains of Tennessee. Throughout his teenage years, Alvin lived a wild life of drinking and gambling. His wild days ended when he gave his life to the Lord at a revival service in the little country church of his mother, in the Valley of the Three Forks of the Wolf.

Following his conversion, Alvin was a pacifist, after the teaching of his church. But when World War I broke out, Alvin received notice from his government that he had to register for the draft. He applied for conscientious objector status, but his application was denied. After much prayer, Scripture reading, and long talks with his pastor, Alvin York decided that he had no choice but to be obedient to the government and accept his country's call into the Army.

Alvin kept a diary, written in the same plain, backwoodsy style in which he spoke. In his diary, he recorded how hard he tried to obey his orders and do what his country told him to do, even though he didn't always agree with or understand those orders:

> I was called the first morning of my army life, to police up in the yard all the old cigarette butts, and I

thought that was pretty hard as I didn't smoke. But I did it just the same.

They gave me a gun and, oh my! that old gun was just full of grease, and I had to clean that old gun for inspection. So I had a hard time to get that old gun clean, and oh, those were trying hours for a boy like me trying to live for God and do His blessed will. But the Lord helped me to bear my hard tasks.

With the rank of corporal, Alvin York was shipped to France with the 82nd "All-American" Infantry Division. There, in the Argonne Forest, York and sixteen other men were ordered to take out a German machine gun emplacement that had killed many American soldiers and stopped the advance of the regiment. York's patrol went behind German lines, and encountered heavy rifle and machine-gun fire. Six men were killed and three were seriously wounded, including the sergeant who was leading the patrol. Suddenly, Corporal York was in command.

While the rest of the survivors took up defensive positions, Alvin York attacked alone. He moved up the ridge, advanced toward the machine-gun nest, and in the process he single-handedly killed twenty-five German soldiers and silenced the gun. He also captured a German major and "persuaded" him at gunpoint that it was in his best interests to order his men to surrender. York returned to his own lines with 132 prisoners (including three high-ranking officers) in tow. He was later promoted to sergeant and given the Congressional Medal of Honor and the Croix de Guerre with Palm. His story was dramatized in the motion picture *Sergeant York*, with Gary Cooper in the title role.

"I never wanted to kill anyone," York later recalled. "I had been living for God and doing church work before I got called for the army. But I thought about it and I reckoned God wanted me to do what the army said, so I just followed orders the best I could. When they told us to take out that machine gun nest, I reckoned we just had to find some way to do it, and so we did. It was a hard battle, and I know God helped me out in that battle, for the bushes were shot off all around me and I never got a scratch. God will be with you if you will only trust Him. I know He saved me back there in France." Alvin York did not question his superior officers. He was obedient to *their* ommands and won a stunning victory.

We may not always agree with or understand God's call upon our lives. Joshua probably didn't. Sometimes God's strategy will call us to do things that seem impossibly hard or even nonsensical, things that will go against our grain. But God is our Commander-in-Chief. Victory requires our absolute obedience. Faith expressed in obedience to God's Word is always the key to success.

What is your "Jericho"—the menacing obstacle that blocks your path right now? What is the "enemy" that has halted your journey toward spiritual wholeness? Is there a sinful habit that you can't seem to break? Is there a hidden shame that keeps you from feeling forgiven? Is there a craving for materialism or worldly success or recognition that keeps you from feeling satisfied with your life? Is it a problem that is at least partly your own doing, such as a financial failure or a difficult marriage relationship? Or is it a circumstance that is completely beyond your control, such as a personal or business calamity, the opposition of other people, or health problems?

Victory over the "Jerichos" in our lives comes only as we learn to trust and obey. We may not understand God's methods and plans, but we can always submit our ways to His will, even with our limited understanding. The conquest of the temptations and obstacles in our lives lies in submission and obedience to God's sovereign leadership. As Paul wrote in 2 Corinthians 10:4, "The weapons of our warfare are not of the flesh, but divinely powerful for the destruction of fortresses."

The Sequence of the Conquest of Jericho (6:8–21)

Shortly after dawn, a long procession began to wind out of the camp of Israel. First came the armed men, marching under tribal banners; then seven priests with trumpets; next the ark of God, and lastly the rear guard. Although the army was prominent in the procession, Jericho would not fall through the might of an army, but by the power of God.

In silence, the procession made its way toward Jericho, winding around the city like a serpent. The city of Jericho covered about nine acres, so the march took about twenty-five to thirty-five minutes to complete. They marched their course in silence—and an eerie, frightening silence it must have seemed to the people in the city. When the circuit was completed, the Israelites would quietly return to camp. They did this once a day for six days.

We are compelled to ask, "Why this seemingly irrational strategy?" No other fortress in history was ever conquered this way. But we can discern at least three reasons for God's strange strategy for the conquest of Jericho:

1. The strategy was designed to test the faith of Joshua—and Joshua passed the test with flying colors. He did not question; he trusted and obeyed.

Here is another "leadership secret" from the leadership model of Joshua: *A true Christian leader must be able to take orders as well as give them.* Those who cannot obey are not qualified to lead. And the One whose orders are to be obeyed above all else, without questioning or hesitation, is God Himself.

Gen. George S. Patton had a unusual way of selecting leaders for promotion. He would line up his candidates and say, "Men, I want a trench dug behind that warehouse. Dig it eight feet long, three feet wide—and *six inches deep.*" Then the general would leave the men to their work. Unknown to them, however, he would go to a room in the warehouse, next to where the digging tools were kept. As the men were getting out the tools to dig the trench, Patton could hear every word they said.

Some complained that this is demeaning work for a lieutenant, or that the trench should be dug by power equipment. Others would gripe about having to dig a stupid, pointless trench in such lousy weather. Others would argue about why in the world the general would want a trench only six inches deep. But finally, one of the men would say, "Who cares what the old so-and-so wants to do with this trench? Let's dig it and get it over with!" And that was the man Patton would promote.

God, too, is looking for leaders who can follow orders and get the job done. It is the Joshua-like leaders who demonstrate a willingness to *take* orders whom God will ultimately promote and entrust with the responsibility to *give* orders.

2. God's strategy was also designed to test Israel's obedience to the will of God. And that was not easy in this situation, for they exposed themselves daily for an entire week, to ridicule and even danger. It appears that Israel, like Joshua, also passed the test. The people trusted—and they obeyed. They seemed to understand that victory depended upon absolute, unquestioning obedience of God's orders.

History remembers Field Marshal Bernard "Monty" Montgomery of Great Britain as an autocratic and relentless military commander. Winston Churchill once characterized him as "indomitable in retreat; invincible in advance; insufferable in victory." He was also the military strategist who defeated Hitler's seemingly unbeatable "Desert Fox," Gen. Erwin Rommel, on the sands of El Alamein, Africa, in 1942.

When Monty took command of British forces in North Africa, his first task was to uncover the cause of the string of humiliating losses Britain had received at the hands of Rommel's desert forces. He soon found it. "Previously, orders had been questioned by subordinates right down the line," said Monty. "I was determined to stop this state of affairs at once." Under Montgomery, orders were no longer questioned. They were *obeyed*. At that point, the tide of battle in North Africa began to turn.

We see the same principle at work in the siege of Jericho. Joshua and his soldiers were on the verge of an important victory—not because of superior war machines or a textbook strategy or strength of numbers, but *because they followed orders*. They didn't argue or question. They didn't revise or improvise. They *obeyed*.

It appears that the Israelites were given orders on a daily basis, so that their obedience was not a once-for-all matter, but a new challenge every morning. That is the way God generally deals with you and me, too. We live today with little or no knowledge of tomorrow. As Alexander Maclaren comments,

> [God] does not open His whole hand at once. He opens a finger at a time, as you do sometimes with your children when you are trying to coax them to take something out of your palm. He gives us enough light for the

moment. He says, "March around Jericho; and be sure that I mean something. What I do mean I will tell you someday." And so we have to put all into His hands.[2]

The faith of the sons of Israel triumphed over fear of enemy attack, ridicule and scorn. Never before and seldom after this historic event did the barometer of faith rise so high in Israel.

3. Finally, God's plan was designed to strike fear into the hearts of the inhabitants of Jericho—and it succeeded in that aim as well. As the Israelites continued their solemn, daily march, the sneers of ridicule faded from their enemies' lips. Soon the people of Jericho were asking each other, "What new type of strategy is this? When and how will they attack?"

On the fateful seventh day, the procession made the circuit of the wall seven times. At the end of the seventh circuit, Joshua's voice rang out clearly, "Shout, for the Lord has given you the city!" The priests gave a blast on the trumpets, the people shouted—and what a shout it was! Imagine all the days of suppressed emotion and adrenal energy the people must have poured into that one great, resounding shout. It was a shout that echoed through the surrounding hills. Wild creatures must have scrambled from their dens and birds must have taken flight at the sound of that shout. The citizens of Jericho undoubtedly fell to their knees at the sound of that shout. The air was rent as if by a sonic boom.

Then the miracle happened: Obedient to the sovereign will of God, the walls of Jericho toppled into ruin!

Instantly, the men of Israel converged on the now-defenseless city. They scrambled over great fallen chunks of debris and found the inhabitants of the city paralyzed with fear, unable to resist. The Israelites proceeded to carry out the awful but necessary work that God had given them to do: they slaughtered every human and animal inhabitant of the city—except Rahab and her household.

Instruments of Holy Judgment

It is clear from the context that Israel carried out this grisly work on God's express command. The ultimate responsibility for the slaughter rested with God, not with the Israelites. The people of Israel were acting not on their own authority, but as instruments of holy, divine judgment.

Jericho was placed under the ban, which meant that Jericho and all its contents would be devoted to Jehovah as the firstfruits of the land. This signified that Israel would receive all of Canaan from Him. No booty was to be taken by the people. In the execution of the ban, men and animals were to be killed. Art objects and utensils would be destroyed, or would be consecrated and set apart for the purposes of the sanctuary.

It is important to remember that God has the right to judge people and nations. The idolatrous worship and licentious lifestyle, so clearly attested by archaeological discoveries, demonstrate that God's judgment of Jericho and the rest of Canaanite society was completely just.

God's purpose was to bless the nation of Israel in the land and to use the Jewish people as a means of blessing the world. But this blessing would be greatly hindered if Israel were infected by the degenerate religion of the Canaanites. Sin is desperately infectious. As Gleason Archer pointedly states,

> In view of the corrupting influence of the Canaanite religion, especially with its religious prostitution . . . and infant sacrifice, it was impossible for pure faith and worship to be maintained in Israel except by the complete elimination of the Canaanites themselves.[3]

In the destruction of Jericho, we discover another "leadership secret" in the example of Joshua: *Never compromise or flirt with sin.* Compromise with evil will destroy a Christian leader. It will create disaster in your spiritual life, your relationships, your business life, and your ministry. It will ruin your reputation. It will affect the behavior and infect the faith of people around you. Sin is a deadly disease and it is extremely contagious. Wherever you find sin in your life, root it out, destroy it, deal with it fully and decisively. If there are temptations in your life, don't flirt with them; put them completely out of sight and out of reach.

Charles Haddon Spurgeon told the story of a lady who advertised for a chauffeur. Three men applied for the job. In the interview, each applicant was asked just one question: "How close could you drive to the edge of a precipice without losing control?"

One answered, "Within six inches."

The next said, "To within a hairbreadth of the edge."

The third one replied, "Lady, if you want a daredevil for a driver, I am not your man. My policy has always been to keep as far away from danger as possible."

The third man got the job!

In the same way, flirting with sin is dangerous. This is why God commanded the destruction of Jericho and why He expects Christians today to judge sin in their lives.

What Toppled the Walls?

One question demands an answer: Why did the walls of Jericho fall at the *exact* moment when the people shouted? Did an earthquake occur and cause the destruction? Were Israelite soldiers secretly undermining the walls while the others marched? Did vibrations set up by the trumpet blasts and the soldiers' shouts bring about the collapse? Were shock waves, caused by the marching feet of the Israelites, responsible?

The narrative leaves little room for such speculations. It is clear from the fact that the walls were completely destroyed—except the small portion supporting Rahab's house!—that *this was a supernaturally caused and controlled event.* Must we know the means by which God brings about His miracles? If the mechanism behind His miracles were explained to us, would we even understand? The truth is simple: In our limited understanding, we cannot go beyond the attitude expressed by the writer to the Hebrews, who wrote, "By faith the walls of Jericho fell down, after they had been encircled for seven days."[4]

Archaeological evidence for the collapse of Jericho's walls in Joshua's day is not as clear as was once supposed. Further excavations have determined that in its long history, Jericho has had thirty-four walls. It is estimated that the area suffered about four earthquakes a century. The thoroughness of Joshua's destruction of the city, and the process of erosion over five centuries until it was refortified in Ahab's time, also contribute to the meager remains and the extreme difficulty of relating these remains to the time of Joshua's attack.

The most significant evidence seems to be the extensive pottery remains found on the mound and in the tombs of the area, pointing to occupancy of Jericho until about 1,400 B.C. Under the pottery is a thick burned layer of ash representing a major destruction to be identified with that of Joshua who had destroyed and burned the city. (For an excellent discussion of the archeology of Old Testament Jericho, see Leon Wood, *A Survey of Israel's History,* Zondervan, pp. 94–99.)

The Sequel to the Conquest of Jericho (6:22–27)

Joshua kept the promise made to Rahab by the two spies. He sent those young men to the house where the scarlet cord hung from the window. She must have greeted them joyfully, following them without hesitation to the appointed place outside the doomed city. Rahab and her family were Gentiles, so they were in need of ceremonial cleansing. The men had to be circumcised before they could be identified with the people of Israel.

Rahab's history is a remarkable example of the grace of God operating in the life of an individual and a family. Regardless of her past life, she was saved by faith in the living God and even became a part of the ancestry of Jesus the Messiah! (See Matt. 2:5). In keeping with the biblical pattern, this believing woman and her family were spared when divine judgment descended on her society. The same was true for Noah and his family, and for Lot and his family. Today, believers can still rejoice in the fact that when God is ready to pour out judgment upon the earth during the coming Great Tribulation, He will first deliver His own to a place of safety. As the apostle Paul affirms in 2 Thessalonians 5:9, "For God has not destined us for wrath, but for obtaining salvation through our Lord Jesus Christ."

The story of Rahab also elevates the position of women and demonstrates that a woman can be a saving blessing to her own family. As one Christian writer explains,

> Men, as heads of their households, are responsible for a family's spiritual welfare, but women have been committed a share in that responsibility and frequently discharge it more faithfully than their husbands. Timothy's mother and grandmother may have had more influence on him than his father. Monica, mother of

99

Augustine, wrestled in prayer in behalf of her wayward son and gave the world one of Christendom's great theologians. Wives, mothers, sisters, aunts, and grandmothers—all may exert great influence, through godly living and faithful prayer, on husbands, sons, brothers, nephews, and grandsons.[5]

Jericho's placement under the ban included the pronouncement of a curse on anyone who would dare to refortify the city by rebuilding a wall around it. Though the site was apparently occupied for brief periods, the anathema was not violated until the days of King Ahab, 500 years later. As a sign of the apostasy of that period, Hiel the Bethelite attempted to rebuild Jericho's walls. This violation of God's judgment upon Jericho directly cost Hiel the lives of his two sons (1 Kings 16:34).

Walking by Faith

The secret to success at Jericho was not Joshua's military genius or the army's skill in warfare. Victory came because the leaders and the people fully trusted God and obeyed His commands. "So the Lord was with Joshua," concludes verse 27, "and his fame was in all the land."

Both then and now, that is what walking by faith is about: trusting God, obeying his commands, and watching Him act in miraculous ways. We all face "Jerichos" at one time or another in our lives, and we too can see the walls crumble as we trust God for victory, as we walk by faith in an invincible God. Dr. Richard Halverson, former chaplain of the U.S. Senate, explains walking by faith this way:

Walking by faith means walking not by sight. Does this mean that one walks blindly?

No more than the pilot of a 747 flies blind when he is being talked into a landing by the control tower.

No more than when a pilot believes his instruments rather than the seat of his pants.

One of the hard lessons a pilot learns is to trust his instruments when they disagree with his feelings.

He is in much greater danger by depending on his feeling than by depending upon his instruments.

Ceiling zero—visibility zero—very poor conditions to fly by sight. . . .

But the aircraft lands safely when the pilot listens to the word from the control tower and obeys it.

To walk by faith is to heed the Word of God . . . to read it, to know it, to learn it, to obey it.

It isn't those who walk by faith that louse up their lives. . . . Rather it is those who walk by sight!

Jesus said, "I am the Light of the world. He who follows Me shall not walk in darkness, but shall have the Light of life" (John 8:23).[6]

If the Israelites had walked by sight, they never would have marched around the city for seven days. They wouldn't have shouted or blown the trumpet. They wouldn't have withstood the risk of Canaanite arrows, the jeers, and the ridicule for seven days. And they wouldn't have seen the walls fall down.

If the Israelites had walked by sight, they would have reconnoitered and planned and strategized. They would have studied the classic city sieges of the past, and they would have attempted to duplicate the winning tactics of other great generals in history. They would have built siege engines and catapults and battering rams and they would have tried to penetrate the gates and walls of the city. They would have lost hundreds, perhaps thousands of brave soldiers. And they would have likely lost the battle.

What about the "Jericho" in your life? Are you attacking it by human wisdom, employing human tactics, using human weapons wielded by human strength? No wonder you are finding the conquest of your "Jericho" impossible! It's time for obedience, time to put away temptation, time to listen to God and ask Him what He commands you to do.

The walls of your "Jericho" are strong and high and well-defended. You cannot climb them or penetrate them by your own strength, but if you follow God's strategy for conquest, then soon, in His perfect timing, they will fall at a single shout!

QUESTIONS FOR REFLECTION AND DISCUSSION

See Your Own Reflection

1. Honestly assess your attitude as you face the battles of your life: Are you on the Lord's side, a soldier in His battle, taking your marching orders from Him? Or are you fighting your own battles and trying to coax God into helping you as you fight the battle on your own terms?

Dig a Little Deeper

2. Examine the various elements of God's strategy for the siege of Jericho. Explain why, in your opinion, these events or aspects were important:

• Joshua's private visit from the man with the sword.

• The silent march around the city.

• The number seven—seven priests, seven trumpets, and the seven circuits of the city on the seventh day.

•The presence of the Ark of the Covenant.

3. In this miracle, we see a cooperation between God's action and human action. The people are commanded to circle the city, to blow the trumpets, to shout—and then God topples the walls. When the walls fall, it is time again for people to act, and to obediently carry out God's judgment on the city.

There are many other situations in Scripture where miracles take place through a combination of divine and human activity. Jesus turned water into wine at Cana—but only after the servants obediently filled the jars with water (John 2). Jesus called Lazarus out of the tomb, still wrapped in grave-clothes—but then He told the friends of Lazarus to go to him and unbind him (John 11).

What does this account say to you about our role in God's eternal plan? Are there situations in your life, either past or present, where you can see that God has made you a partner in the performance of His miracles?

4. What does the total destruction of Jericho say to you about how God views sin?

5. "A true Christian leader," says Dr. Campbell, "must be able to take orders as well as give them. Those who cannot obey are not qualified to lead." As a person who seeks to be a better Christian leader, how good are you at taking orders from God (on a scale of 1 to 10)?

How good are you at taking orders from your superiors in your ministry, your business, or the military (on a scale of 1 to 10)?

Explain your answers and cite recent examples and experiences from your own life.

Let's Get Personal

6. God's strategy for the conquest of Jericho must have been baffling to Joshua and his people. What one aspect of God's operation in your life today do you find completely baffling? How are you responding to God's mysterious ways in your life?

7. What is your "Jericho" today—the menacing obstacle that blocks your path right now? What is the "enemy" that has halted your journey toward spiritual wholeness?"

What do you feel God would have you do to conquer the "Jericho" in your life?

6

THE AGONY OF DEFEAT

JOSHUA 7–8

It was probably the most shocking upset in the history of football.

The Washington Redskins had been the dominant team in the NFL throughout the entire decade, and were heavily favored over all rivals as they entered the 1940 season. As the big game against the Chicago Bears approached, oddsmakers favored Washington to win by 14 points. But from the moment the opening gun fired, things began to go wrong for the Redskins.

While the Redskins fumbled, bumbled, and stumbled, the Bears surged over the gridiron like an unstoppable force. Near the end of the fourth quarter, the Bears had rolled over the Redskins for six touchdowns, a field goal, and a safety, and the Redskins—the odds-on favorites—had not scored a single touchdown! The score stood at 73 to 0.

But in the last remaining seconds, just before the final gun, the Redskins made one valiant 75-yard drive. The Bears stopped them on the *six-inch line!* First down, just six more inches to go! The Redskins were determined not to leave the field without at least one touchdown to their credit. The team came out of the huddle and hit the line of scrimmage. The ball was snapped, the Redskins star quarterback, Sammy Baugh, went back to pass, he fired the ball to a wide-open receiver in the end-zone—

Suddenly, a Chicago defensive back appeared out of nowhere, cutting across the end-zone and snatching the ball out of the air! Interception! Seconds later, the final gun sounded. The game was over, and the score was still 73 to zip! To this day, that game is remembered as one of the most humiliating surprise defeats in the annals of football history.

In a similar but much more tragic and costly way, Israel—the odds-on favorite in the battle for the Promised Land—suffered a stunning upset, a totally unexpected defeat when its army went up against the city of Ai. Prior to Ai, Joshua and his army had experienced only victory. After the smashing triumph over Jericho, the Israelites had put all thought of defeat out of their minds. They saw themselves as invulnerable—yet God's people are never more vulnerable, never in greater danger, than right after winning a great victory. For then they are susceptible to pride and complacency.

Ai, the next obstacle in the path of Israel, was a smaller fortress than Jericho, but heavily defended. It was strategically located on the eastern edge of Canaan's central ridge. The defeat of Ai would give the Israelites command of the hill country and control of the route from Gilgal into the interior.

Archaeologists have often identified Ai with the site now known as et-Tell. Excavations show, however, that this site was not occupied during the period between 2,400 and 1,200 B.C. When Joshua and his army were engaged in the conquest of the region in 1,400 B.C., the site at et-Tell was already in ruins. The exact location of Ai is yet to be determined. Though we are not able to sift the ruins of Ai, we can observe the importance of what took place there from the amount of biblical material given to a discussion of Israel's defeat—and later victory—at Ai.

Defeat at Ai (7:1–26)

Jericho had been placed under God's ban, so that every living thing in the city had to be put to death, and valuable objects were to be dedicated to the Lord's treasury. No Israelite soldier was permitted to take any of the booty for himself. But that temptation proved too strong for a man named Achan.

In this passage we see the six-stage course of events surrounding the defeat at Ai. Those six stages were:

1. Disobedience
2. Defeat
3. Dismay
4. Directions
5. Discovery
6. Death.

Let's examine each of these stages in turn:

1. Disobedience (7:1)

A seminary professor was once counseling a couple who had severe marital problems. When the seminary professor suggested they spend more time in prayer about their problems, the husband protested, "We certainly don't want the Lord to know about this!" But the Lord knows everything that happens, everything we do, everything we think. And the Lord knew about the sin of Achan.

Alexander Whyte has drawn a dramatic picture of the disobedience and downfall of Achan:

> Who is that stealing about among the smoking ruins? Is that some soldier of Jericho who has saved himself from the devouring sword? When the night wind wakens the embers again, these are the accoutrements and movements of one of Joshua's men. Has he lost his way? Has he been half dead, and has he not heard the rally of the trumpet? He hides, he listens, he looks through the darkness, he disappears into the darkness.[1]

We might be inclined to applaud the discipline of Joshua's forces. After all, *only one* of his thousands of soldiers gave way to temptation! But that one soldier did not escape God's notice. Sin never escapes the watchful eye of God.

Not only did God see Achan's sin, but because of it, His anger burned against the entire nation. He considered the people collectively responsible, and He withheld His blessing until the matter was set right. In fact, a careful reading of the Lord's words to Joshua suggests that Israel's history would have ended right then and there if God had not turned away from His anger.

2. Defeat (7:2–5)

Unaware of Achan's disobedience and eager to take advantage of the momentum generated by Israel's first victory, Joshua made preparations for the next battle by sending spies ten miles northwest to Ai. When the spies returned, they spoke with great confidence: "If you think Jericho fell with ease, wait until we get to Ai. We can conquer them easily with two or three thousand men!"

But the spies were wrong. When God gave the orders to Joshua, He told them to take "all the people of war" (8:1). Though not as large as Jericho, Ai was well-fortified and her soldiers were well-entrenched. The Israelites were guilty of underestimating the defenses of Ai, and of overestimating their own strength. As you read this passage, you find no mention of prayer, consecration, or dependence upon God.

Underestimating your enemy is a fatal failing, whether on the battlefield, the sports field, the field of business, or the field of spiritual warfare. In his business bestseller *What They Don't Teach You at Harvard Business School,* entrepreneur Mark H. McCormack tells a story which is a modern parable of what can happen in any of these fields when you understimate your opponent. He was playing doubles on a tennis court in Geneva, and one of his opponents was the famed tennis star Bjorn Borg. McCormack and Borg were squared off from each other just a few feet on either side of the net. Borg's partner hit a soft lob to McCormack, and McCormack—supremely confident—saw that Borg would be completely defenseless against a hard overhand smash.

"For the briefest of split seconds," McCormack recalls, "I thought it would be unfair to hit the ball directly at him. I did anyway, of course. I smashed the ball right at his midsection—and Borg promptly whistled it past my head for a winning point." McCormack's rueful moral: "Never underestimate your competition."[2]

The Israelites made the same mistake at Ai that McCormack made on the tennis court: They were supremely confident, they assumed their opponent was wide-open and defenseless, and they went for the surprise overhand smash—only to discover that the surprise was on them! In the defeat of Israel at Ai, we can find another "leadership secret" of Joshua—one that Joshua and the people learned the hard way: *Never underestimate the enemy or overestimate yourself.* Christians are often guilty of underrating the enemy's power—and they fall into ignominious defeat as a consequence!

Who or what is your "enemy" right now? Is it a sinful habit that threatens to overwhelm you? Is it a major obstacle that blocks your business or ministry plans? Is it a bout of paralyzing, immobilizing depression? Is it that official at the city planning department who refuses to give your church or business permission to expand the parking lot? Is it that manipulative, obstructionist member of your church board who aggressively undermines your ministry and blocks every move you make? Is it a struggle with temptation, lust, or greed? Is it the tendency toward materialism, pride, ambition, or compulsive workaholism—all tendencies which our society applauds but which can destroy our usefulness to God? Or is your enemy in fact *the Enemy*, Satan himself, who seeks to drag us down and rob us of our effectiveness as a soldier of the Lord?

Whatever our "enemy," we dare not underestimate that "enemy's" power to defeat us. We dare not underestimate the power of Satan. We dare not underestimate the power of temptation, sin, and the addictions and compulsions that so easily bind us. We dare not underestimate the power of our inner blind spots and character flaws to blunt our effectiveness for God. When these "enemies" are bigger than we are we should be courageous enough to admit our inadequacy, set aside our pride, and seek help—from God, from other Christians, from a Christian counselor or pastor, or from a Christian accountability group, fellowship group, or support group.

If our "enemy" is a human enemy, then we must be careful not to give in to hate. We must love our enemy, as Christ commanded us—but that doesn't mean we have to blindly *trust* that enemy! We should treat those who oppose us and our Gospel with care and watchfulness. We should be, as Jesus said, "shrewd as serpents, and innocent as doves."[3] In other words, don't hate anyone, don't hurt anyone—but don't underestimate anyone either.

The calamity which befell Israel was due, at least in part, to minimizing the enemy and to assuming that one victory guaranteed another. It simply doesn't work that way. Yesterday's victory does not make us immune from defeat today. There must be continual dependence upon the Lord for strength. As Paul wrote, "Be strong in the Lord, and in the strength of His might."[4]

Euphoric over their victory at Jericho, Joshua and the Israelites sent only 3,000 men to Ai. Instead of conquering, Joshua's forces were routed and humiliated. Terrorized by the forces of Ai, they were chased through the same steep mountain pass they had climbed so confidently that morning. In that rugged country, thirty-six of the Israelite soldiers were caught and killed by the fierce and merciless warriors of Ai. Those who returned to the Israelite camp brought a story of defeat and shame.

After the amazing miracle at the Jordan and the easy triumph over Jericho, the entire camp was bewildered and demoralized by this disastrous turn of events. "The hearts of the people melted," says verse 5, "and became as water." The most significant issue in this event was not the defeat itself, nor even the thirty-six unfortunate men who lost their lives among the rocks below Ai. The real issue here is that Israel was suddenly filled with terrible doubts and misgivings. Jehovah's help had been withdrawn, seemingly without reason. What had happened? Had God changed His mind?

3. Dismay (7:6–9)

Joshua was as stunned by the defeat as the rest of the Israelites. In keeping with the ancient rites of mourning, he and the elders tore their clothes, put dust on their heads, and fell on their faces before the Ark of the Lord. They stayed there, mourning this loss, until evening. Then Joshua put his doubts and confusion into words, in the form of three anguished questions (verses 7–9, NIV):

• "Why did You ever bring this people across the Jordan, to deliver us into the hands of the Amorites to destroy us? If only we had been content to stay on the other side of the Jordan!"

• "What can I say, now that Israel has been routed by its enemies? The Canaanites . . . will hear about this and they will surround us and wipe out our name from the earth."

• "What then will You do for Your own great name?"

At first it appeared that Joshua was blaming God for the defeat, and not even considering that the cause might lie with his own people. He even adopted the thinking of the spies whom Moses sent into Canaan, against whom he had so vehemently protested at Kadesh-barnea. They had said, "would that we had died in the land of Egypt! Or would that we had died in this wilderness! And why is the Lord bringing us into this land, to fall by the sword? Our wives and our little ones will become plunder."[5]

In fact, however, we see by close examination of Joshua's words that his overriding emotion is not self-pity or bitterness against God, but a concern that the news of this defeat might cause God's own name to be dishonored among the heathen. His reactions show us how very human he was, and we feel a strong kinship with this man as he pours out his honest hurt and confusion before God. In our own dark moments of discouragement, defeat, and depression, every one of us has experienced feelings like Joshua's. We, too, easily forget the promises and the previous victories of our God. In those dark times, we all too often forget the truths God has revealed to us in the light.

4. Directions (7:10–15)

The Lord's reply to Joshua was blunt: "Rise up! Why is it that you have fallen on your face?" God proceeded to explain the cause of the defeat and the need for action. The cause of the disaster was with Israel, not with God—for Israel had sinned. Then God delivered the indictment by means of what Alexander Maclaren has called an "indignant accumulation of verbs." Moving from the general to the particular, Israel was charged by God with sin, with breaching the covenant, with appropriating items which were placed under the ban, with stealing and deceiving and concealing stolen goods. Until these transgressions were repudiated and an atonement made, the sin of the one transgressor—Achan—would be considered the sin of the entire nation.

In effect, God said to Joshua, "Don't you remember what caused the defeat of Israel at Kadesh? Don't you remember what caused Israel's subsequent wanderings for thirty-eight years in the wilderness? Sin has once again come among My people, and that is why you should not be here on your face. This is not time for prayer, but for action. Go back to the camp and deal with this sin!"

After the fall of Jericho, it was recorded, "So the Lord was with Joshua" (Josh. 6:27). But now a different announcement came from the mouth of God: He would not be with Joshua unless the sin was judged. As Wesley Hunt observed,

> Sin causes the loss of God's presence and power. Sin shuts off the showers of God's blessing. Sin stifles and strangles the abundant life promised in Jesus Christ. Sin paralyzes and immobilizes the life of the

individual believer and of the local body. God's message to Joshua applies also to God's people today in times of obvious spiritual defeat and decline; namely, deal with sin![6]

Many years ago, as the student pastor of a small church I was baffled by the lack of visible growth and the seeming absence of God's blessing. One Sunday a young woman offered her resignation as a Sunday School teacher, explaining that she too was concerned about the condition of the church—and feared that she was the cause of it! She confessed that she felt she was the "Achan in the camp."

We do not part with sin easily. Augustine, in a revealing passage of his *Confessions*, admitted that as a young man he often prayed, "O God, give me chastity—but not yet." Perhaps you identify with the younger Augustine. You know that there are habits you must give up, sins you must repent of, and you really want to make those changes in your life—but not quite yet. You want to enjoy them just a little longer.

Suppose that when Jesus went to the woman possessed by seven demons and offered to cast them out, she had said, "Yes, Lord, but may I ask a favor? Will You cast out six and leave just one? I'm just not quite ready to give up all my demons right now." Preposterous, right? But if you wouldn't cling to a demon, why would you cling to a sin or a self-destructive habit?

One man, Achan, defiled the whole camp. And one sinful habit defiles the man. There can be no temporizing or compromising with sin. Judgment must be decisive and complete. An authentic Christian leader is someone whose secret inner self is seamlessly joined to his outer self, someone whose inner reality equals or exceeds his reputation. As Howard Hendricks has said, "You show me a leader who is great in public and I will show you a leader who is even greater in private."

There is a word for the quality Howard Hendricks is talking about—a quality that was sadly lacking in the life of Achan. That word is *integrity.* Integrity is a key ingredient for effective leadership in every arena of life: in the home, in government, in the military, in the church, and in business.

Though many people view the business world as a dog-eat-dog, anything-for-a-buck environment, management expert Tom Peters says that in business, as in every other arena of life, leaders should *demand total integrity* of themselves and of their employees. In the concluding chapter of his book *Thriving on Chaos*—a chapter aptly entitled "Demand Total Integrity"—Peters writes,

> Without doubt, honesty has always been the best policy. The best firms on this score have long had the best track records overall—Johnson & Johnson, IBM, S.C. Johnson (Johnson Wax), Hewlett-Packard, Merck, Digital Equipment. . . . Integrity means living up to commitments, inside and outside the firm. In a world of exploding product and service offerings, keeping your word takes on added significance. . . .
>
> High quality of product and high quality of service demand absolute integrity. . . . Superior quality simply cannot be extracted from a low-integrity organization. . . .
>
> There is no such thing as a minor lapse in integrity. IBM has been known to fire an employee for accepting a gratuity from a supplier (a pen set), and then discipline the employee's boss severely as well. . . . I believe that such rigid behavior around "little" integrity issues is a must.[7]

Ron Willingham, author of *Integrity Selling*, also touts the importance of integrity in business. "Who I am communicates!" he writes. "Sooner or later, most people will get the message about the level of integrity I have. And they often get the message pretty quickly."[8] Willingham and Peters agree: Integrity is a key ingredient for success.

Integrity exalts us; sin dooms us. We cannot hope to succeed on the spiritual battlefield, on the ministry battlefield, or even on the business battlefield so long as there is a little bit of Achan lurking around inside us. The sin in our lives must be dealt with, fully and decisively.

In verses 13 through 15, God lays out the steps for purging Israel of the sin which keeps the nation in a state of defeat:

1. The people were to sanctify themselves.

2. On the next day, the people were to gather for the identification of the offender—presumably by the casting of lots.

3. The culprit was to be destroyed, because he had "committed a disgraceful thing in Israel."

5. Discovery (7:16–21)

Joshua rose early on the fateful day. All Israel was assembled for the sacred ritual of drawing lots. The method probably called for the selecting of inscribed shards of pottery out of a jar. Since God knew who was guilty, why didn't He simply reveal the identity to Joshua? God probably chose this more dramatic method of revealing the culprit for two reasons: 1. To impress upon the nation of Israel the seriousness of disobedience. 2. To give the guilty person an opportunity to repent. If Achan had responded this way, confessing rather than hiding his guilt, he would no doubt have been pardoned, just as David was pardoned for his sin centuries later.

There was grim silence in the camp as the lots were cast. Each successive casting of the lots narrowed the list of suspects. The first lot was cast, selecting the tribe of Judah. Another lot, selecting the family of the Zerhrites. Another, selecting the household of Zabdi. Another, and Achan himself was indicated. This was no mere coincidence or quirk of fate. This was the movement of the finger of God among human affairs. As Solomon once wrote, "The lot is cast into the lap; but its every decision is from the Lord."[9]

Strangely, Achan remained silent throughout the entire procedure. Surely his heart must have pounded and his stomach must have churned with fear as the lots fell closer and closer to his own doorstep. Finally, Joshua stood before Achan and addressed him, tenderly but firmly. Though Joshua hated the sin, he did not despise the sinner. A public confession was needed to confirm that the supernatural exposure of Achan was indeed just and accurate.

Achan's response was straightforward and complete. He confessed his sin and made no excuses. But nowhere in his response do we find an expression of sorrow for having disobeyed God's command, nor for having betrayed his nation, nor for causing the defeat of Israel, nor for causing the deaths of thirty-six brave Hebrew soldiers.

The three steps to destruction that Achan took are familiar: he saw, he coveted, he took. Eve followed the same destructive path in the Garden of Eden.[10] And David followed this same destructive path in his adultery with Bathsheba.[11]

The material objects Achan hid under the floor of his tent included a beautiful mantle (or cloak) of Shinar, an ingot of gold, and some pieces of silver. Achan may well have reasoned, "After all, I have been deprived of the good things of life these many years in the wilderness.

Here is a beautiful new, stylish cloak for me to wear, plus some gold and silver. Why would God want to withhold these things from me? They will never be missed—and I'm entitled to some pleasure and prosperity!'"

But Achan was fooling himself. He knew full well that there was a specific command against taking any of the booty of Jericho for personal use. God's Word can never be rationalized away without penalty.

Achan was caught in a mindset that is as contemporary and relevant to our age as the space shuttle and the computer. He was seduced by *materialism*. Writes Charles Swindoll,

> Believe it or not, the average American is exposed to about three hundred advertisements a day. Personally, I believe it! The magazine in which I read that fact yesterday has more pages dedicated to advertisements than articles of interest to the reader. Shiny, slick, appealing print and pictures designed to hijack your concentration and kidnap your attention. Before you realize it, the Madison Avenue Pied Piper has led you into a world of exaggerated make-believe, convincing you that you simply cannot live without. . .
> • a new Polaroid camera stuffed with SX-70 film (that develops *twice* as fast!)
> • an elegant diamond solitaire (a diamond is *forever!*)
> • a Dodge Sportsman Wagon to pull your new outboard
> • a set of Firestone's finest
> • Carter's Little Pills "specially coated to pass right through your stomach releasing their action only in your lower tract"[12]

Besides the advertising we find in our print and broadcast media, we are exposed to ads whenever we get in our cars and drive past a billboard or a bus-stop. Computer users are exposed to continuous ads whenever they "log on" to the Prodigy computer network. Customers calling businesses are exposed to "ads on hold" while they wait for a human being to pick up the phone. Advertising is ubiquitous, and the one message almost all ads have in common is this: "You can have a complete, fulfilled, satisfied life if you would only drive this car, drink this beverage, or use this hair spray!" That is a message of *materialism*—and it is a seductive and dangerous message.

As Christians, you and I should take a long look at the sin of Achan, then remember Paul's exhortation to put to death the sin of covetousness, "which amounts to idolatry."[13] Satan tempts us to compromise and sin through our desire for material things. Jesus said, "Beware, and be on your guard against every form of greed; for not even when one has an abundance does his life consist of his possessions."[14]

6. Death (7:22–26)

Achan's confession was quickly verified and the stolen objects were retrieved and laid out before the Lord. Then Achan was led out to the Valley of Achor, along with his whole household and his possessions. There, he and his children were stoned to death and their bodies and belongings were consumed by fire. Having stolen objects claimed by God, Achan was contaminated. In view of the fact that the Law prohibits the execution of children for their father's sins,[15] we must assume that Achan's children knew about—and were accomplices in—his crime.

A marker in the form of a great heap of stones was raised over the body of Achan. This seems to have been a common method of burial for infamous people. It served as a warning to all Israel against the sin of disobeying God's commands.

119

Thus Achan, whose name meant "troubler," was buried in the Valley of Achor, the Valley of Troubling. And because Israel was willing to deal with the sin problem, God's anger was turned away from Israel. Once again, God was ready to lead Israel to victory.

William Brodie was a respected man in eighteenth century Edinburgh society. Head of the Incorporation of Edinburgh Wrights and Masons, he was highly skilled in the invention, construction, and maintenance of all sorts of mechanical devices. One of his inventions was a mechanical trapdoor designed to make execution-by-hanging more reliable and efficient. Prior to Brodie's invention, condemned prisoners were simply pushed from the scaffold, and sometimes death was quick and othertimes it was excruciatingly slow. The Brodie trapdoor, however, made short business of virtually every execution. With only minor improvements, Brodie's invention remains in use in many parts of the world today.

What no one knew at the time while Brodie was working on his new and improved killing device was that Brodie himself had an Achan-like secret: *He was one of the busiest burglars in all Scotland!* When his crimes were uncovered, he fled to Holland, but was captured and returned to Edinburgh. There he was tried and condemned to death. On a cold winter's day in 1788, Brodie became a victim of his own invention, when the trapdoor dropped from beneath his bound feet, and he died at the end of a rope.

William Brodie probably never imagined, years earlier when he was building and testing his new and improved execution machine, that it would someday become the means of his own death. And Achan never imagined that his little compromise with sin, his private little entanglement with materialism and theft, would end in the destruction of himself and all he held dear—even his own children. So now the question to you and me is: What acts of sin are we contemplating or committing *right now* which will one day bring us sorrow, humiliating exposure, loss, and death?

The cloak, the gold, and the silver were beautiful to behold, but they only brought destruction to Achan. His terrible end is a sobering reminder to us that "the wages of sin is death,"[16] and that "when lust has conceived, it gives birth to sin; and when sin is accomplished, it brings forth death."[17]

Victory at Ai (8:1–35)

While the American Civil War was raging and the fate of the country hung in the balance, a delegation of northern preachers visited President Lincoln at the White House. "Mr. President," they said, "we want you to be assured that God is on our side."

Lincoln shook his head. "No, my friends," he replied, "rather let us pray that we may be found on *God's* side."

After the defeat at Ai, Joshua may well have wondered if Israel was on God's side or not. But once Achan's crime had been exposed and judged, God's favor toward Israel was again restored. The Lord reassured Joshua that He had not forsaken Joshua or Joshua's people. In verse 1, He said to him, "Do not fear or be dismayed."

When Joshua heard these words, his pulse quickened, for these were the same words Moses had spoken in Kadesh-barnea when he sent out Joshua and the other eleven spies to scout out Canaan.[18] They were also the same words Moses said to Joshua forty years later as he turned the reins of leadership over to the younger man.[19]

Joshua heard those words again from God, just after the death of Moses.[20] Now, at this crucial time in Joshua's life, it was good for him to be reminded and reassured that God was ready to lead—*if* Joshua was ready to listen to *His* plan.

Turning Defeat into Victory

The dividing line between Joshua 7 and Joshua 8 is a dividing line between two sets of contrasts:

Chapter 7	Chapter 8
Israel is defeated	Israel is victorious
One man's sin	One nation's obedience
No prayer before battle	Prayer before battle
Only 3,000 soldiers used	All of Israel's army used
Israel guided by	Israel guided by
Human reason	Divine revelation

Joshua chapter 8 can be divided into three sections as follows:
1. The Setting of the Battle—Verses 1–2
2. The Sequence of the Battle—Verses 3–29
3. The Sequel to the Battle—Verses 30–35

Let's examine, in turn, each step in the conquest of Ai.

1. The Setting of the Battle (8:1–2)

God's plan involved using all the fighting men of Israel. While the primary cause of the defeat at Ai was Achan's sin, the secondary cause was the underrating of the enemy.

The divine plan also included returning to Ai, the place of Israel's humiliating defeat. God said, "Arise, go up to Ai." And He promised to turn the place of Israel's bitter defeat into a place of sweet victory.

Historians tell us of an Italian naval engagement that took place in the sixteenth century between the fleets of two rival city-states, Genoa and Venice. In the battle, the Genoese admiral sustained a crushing defeat, and ordered his ships to retreat. But after repairs to his ships were completed, he ordered his men to set sail for the scene of the former battle.

"What?" asked the officers. "Return to the place where we were routed?"

"Yes," the admiral replied through clenched teeth. "It was rendered famous by our defeat, and I will make it *immortal* by our victory!"

That is the kind of turn-around Israel now sought to achieve—and it is the kind of turn-around you and I can experience after our own defeats in life. Defeat *can* be turned into victory through the power of God. As 1 John 1:9 tells us, whenever our fellowship with God is broken by sin, we can identify the sin, confess it to God, claim His forgiveness, and experience a restored relationship and true *victory* in life.

Before the actual plan of battle was revealed to Joshua, he was told that the spoil of Ai could be taken by Israel. Jericho had been placed under the ban, but Ai was not. In this fact we discover a tragic irony: If only Achan had suppressed his greedy and selfish desires and obeyed God's command at Jericho, he would later have had all the prosperity his heart desired—plus the richness of God's blessing and approval as well! How easy—and how deadly—it is for us to take matters into our own hands and go ahead of the Lord!

2. The Sequence of the Battle (8:3–29)

The order of events at Ai was entirely different from the order of events at Jericho. The Israelites did not march around the walls of Ai seven times, nor did the walls fall miraculously. Israel had to conquer the city through the normal operations of war. There is an important principle illustrated in this fact: *God is not limited to any one method of working*. He is not stereotyped in His operations. He is endlessly creative in how he chooses to work. As Francis Schaeffer writes,

> We Christians should not be surprised when the Holy Spirit leads us in different ways at different times. He will not contradict His own principles or character as set forth in the Scriptures, but He will not act like a machine, always responding to similar situations in exactly the same ways. When a Christian falls into the idea that because Jericho has been taken one way, Ai must be taken the same way, he has stopped thinking of God as personal.[21]

God's strategy for the capture of Ai was ingenious. God instructed Joshua to place an ambush behind the city. The outworking of this plan involved three contingents of soldiers.

The first group of soldiers was the main army which came the fifteen-mile distance from Gilgal early the next morning and camped in plain view on the north side of Ai. Led by Joshua, this army was a diversionary force to decoy the defenders of Ai out of the city.

The second group of soldiers were sent by night to hide just west of the city of Ai. Their assignment was to wait until the defenders left the city to pursue Joshua and his army, then rush into the gates and torch the city. While the text indicates this unit numbered 30,000, this seems an excessively large number of men to hide near the city. Since the Hebrew word translated "thousand" may also be rendered "chief" or "officer," it appears better to view this as a choice group of thirty brave officers chosen by Joshua for a daring commando-type mission.

The third group of soldiers was another ambush unit of 5,000 men who were positioned between Bethel and Ai to cut off the possibility of reinforcements from Bethel to aid the men of Ai.

The plan worked to perfection. When the king of Ai saw Israel's army, he took the bait. Pursuing the Israelites who pretended defeat, the men of Ai left their city unguarded. At Joshua's signal, the commando troops quickly entered and set the city on fire. The men of Ai were thrown into complete panic and confusion as they looked back and saw the flame and smoke billowing up out of their city. Before they could gather their wits, they were caught in the Israelite pincers and slaughtered.

Reentering the city, Israel's army brought death to all of Ai's inhabitants, 12,000 people in all, then Joshua burned the city to the ground. Ai's king was hanged on a tree, then buried beneath a pile of stones. Thus Israel, restored to God's favor, won a great victory. After failure, there was a second chance. We, too, should remember that one defeat or failure does not signal the end of our usefulness for God. We can always learn the lessons of defeat. We can always repent and seek God's forgiveness after a defeat. God in His grace stands ready to restore us and use us again.

3. The Sequel to the Battle (8:30–35)

Following the victory at Ai, Joshua did something that seemed militarily foolish. Instead of moving quickly to achieve further victories and secure the central sector of the land, he led the Israelites on a spiritual pilgrimage. This was the same spiritual exercise that Moses had earlier commanded. (See Deut. 27.)

Without delay Joshua led the men, women, children, and cattle from Gilgal northward, up the Jordan Valley, to the place God specified, the mountains of Ebal and Gerizim, near the city of Shechem. The march of about thirty miles was not difficult or dangerous, since they passed through a very sparsely populated area. But how did the Israelites avoid a confrontation with the men of the city of Shechem? The fortress of Shechem guarded the entrance to the valley between the mountains.

Of course the Bible does not record every battle of the conquest and the record of the capture of Shechem may have been omitted. On the other hand, the city may at this time have been in friendly hands or it may simply have surrendered without resistance. But why was this location chosen? Because these mountains are located in the geographic center of the land and from either peak a great deal of the Promised Land can be seen.

Here, then, in a place which overlooked much of the Promised Land—and thus symbolically represented all of the land—Joshua challenged the people to renew their covenant vows to Jehovah. The solemn and significant religious ceremonies at this location involved three events: (1) the construction of a stone altar; (2) the construction of inscribed stone pillars; and (3) the reading of the Law to the people. Let's examine the significance of each of these events.

1. The construction of a stone altar. An altar of stones was erected on Mt. Ebal and sacrifices were offered to the Lord. Jericho and Ai, in which the false gods of the Canaanites were worshiped, had fallen. Israel had conquered. So the conquering nation honored God by publicly worshipping Him and proclaiming faith in, and allegiance to, the one true God.

2. The construction of inscribed stone pillars. Joshua set up some large stone pillars and on their whitewashed surfaces wrote a copy of the Law of Moses. Just how much of the Law was inscribed cannot be determined. Some suggest that only the Ten Commandments were written there, while others believe it included Deuteronomy chapters 5 through 26. While it might seem unlikely that so much text could be inscribed on a single pillar, there are archaeological precedents. In other Middle Eastern locations, a number of similarly inscribed pillars (called *stelae*) have been found, standing some six to eight feet in height, and containing extremely long inscriptions. For example, the Behistun inscription in Iran is *three times* the length of the book of Deuteronomy.

3. The reading of the Law to the people. Half the people were positioned on the slopes of Mt. Gerizim to the south; the other half were on the slopes of Mt. Ebal to the north. And, surrounded by the Levitical priests, the Ark of the Covenant stood in the valley between the two mountains. This large natural amphitheater made it possible for the people to hear every word.

As the curses of the Law were read one by one, the tribes on Mt. Ebal responded, "Amen!" As the blessings were read, the tribes on Mt. Gerizim responded, "Amen!" (See Deut. 27:12–26.) With all sincerity Israel affirmed that the Law of the Lord was indeed to be the law of the land. Here, as Francis Schaeffer suggests, was a powerfully graphic object lesson that God wanted to impress upon the people. God wanted them to understand, writes Schaeffer, that

> what happened to them in the land was going to depend, as it were, on whether they were living on Mt. Gerizim or Mt. Ebal. The people were to hear from Mt. Gerizim the blessings which would come to them if they kept

God's Law, and from Mt. Ebal the curses that would fall upon them, if they did not.[22]

The history of the Jewish people since that time has been determined by their attitude toward the Law. When obedient, they have experienced the blessing of God. When disobedient, they have experienced judgment. (See Deut. 28.) What a tragedy that the meaning of this object lesson and the affirmations the people made upon those two mountains faded so quickly from their minds!

But have we done any better than those ancient Israelites? Have we been any more faithful to our affirmation of loyalty to God and His Word, either as individuals or as a nation? Is the Law of the Lord the law of our lives? And is it the law of our land?

Admittedly, our pluralistic society is not bound to God in a covenant relationship as ancient Israel was. But the evidence is there for all to see—Christians, Jews, people of other religions, agnostics, atheists, New Agers: The moral precepts from both the Old and New Testaments furnish guidelines for building successful lives and successful nations. The fact that our media and our institutions try to deny the relevance and validity of biblical values does not make them any less true or relevant.

The further we depart from the precepts of Scripture, the worse our individual and national problems grow. Statistics clearly demonstrate that the decline of Judeo-Christian values in America is directly paralleled by an increase in drug abuse, divorce, violence and sexual abuse against children, and all categories of violent crime. As the wise old man of Old Testament times observed, "Righteousness exalts a nation, but sin is a disgrace to any people."[23] And a wise man of our own century, Woodrow Wilson, said this: "Our civilization cannot survive materially unless it is redeemed spiritually."

The survival of our society may well depend on the willingness of all the people, the leaders in Washington and the citizens across the land, to allow the absolutes of God's Word to become the law of the land. And Christians must lead the way. You and I must commit ourselves daily to the task of cleansing and purging the "Achan" from ourselves. We must commit ourselves to becoming people of purity, faith, and integrity, inside and out, publicly and privately. Then—and only then—will we be ready to march against the enemy fortresses that stand in our path—*and win the victory.*

QUESTIONS FOR REFLECTION AND DISCUSSION

See Your Own Reflection

1. Were you ever punished for, or injured by, another person's sin? How did that experience make you feel toward that person?

Dig a Little Deeper

2. As you read the story of Israel's defeat and later victory, with whom do you most identify? (Explain your answer.)

❏ Achan, at the moment of his temptation as he sifts through the rubble of Jericho and finds the treasures.

❏ One of the thirty-six soldiers who is being pursued to death because of another person's sin.

❑ Joshua, feeling bewildered and depressed as he questions God after the defeat.

❑ Achan, after the defeat of Israel, knowing he is the guilty one, watching in horror as the lots fall closer and closer to his own doorstep.

❑ Achan, exposed and ashamed as the sinner in the camp.

❑ Joshua, standing before Achan, having the difficult task of confronting another person's sin.

❑ Joshua at the moment of triumph over Ai.

3. Review Joshua 6:18–19, God's instructions to Israel regarding the destruction of Jericho. Why was God angry with the entire nation of Israel because of one man's sin? How do you feel about God's actions in this account? Was God fair or unfair?

4. Examine Joshua's reaction to the defeat at Ai in his dialogue with God, 7:7–9. Does Joshua have a right to speak this way to God?

5. What attitude do you see in Achan as you read this account? Do you think he was sorry for his sin or sorry he got caught? Why wasn't Achan forgiven after he made his confession?

6. What New Testament event does the story of Achan bring to mind? (See Acts 5.) What parallels do you see between these two stories?

What do these two accounts—Josh. 7–8 and Acts 5—suggest to us about church discipline and the need for accountability and responsibility in the church?

Let's Get Personal

7. If you were Joshua, how would you have dealt with Achan? How do you tend to treat discipline issues at work, at home, or at church? Are you a "show-no-mercy, take-no-prisoners" sort of leader? Are you merciful to the point of being a wimp? Are you somewhere in between?

8. Which of the errors, character flaws, and sins found in this account do you recognize in your own life?

❏ A tendency to overconfidence.

❏ A tendency to prayerlessness when approaching life's challenges and decisions.

❏ A tendency to run ahead of God, or to be impatient with his timing.

❏ A tendency to blame God for your own defeats.

❏ A tendency to despair and give up in the face of defeat rather than to pick yourself up and keep on trying.

❏ A materialistic or covetous attitude.

❏ A tendency to flirt with temptation.

❏ Hidden sins or habits.

7

THE PERIL OF PRAYERLESSNESS

JOSHUA 9–10

In the depths of winter at Valley Forge, George Washington went to his knees in prayer, certain that unless God aided his bedraggled and discouraged army, all hope for the fledgling United States was lost.

During the Civil War, when the fate of the nation again hung in the balance, Abraham Lincoln confessed to a friend that he was often driven to his knees to pray because he had nowhere else to go.

In Joshua 9 and 10, we see the fate of another nation—the nation of Israel—dangling by the slender thread of prayer. Israel's failure to consult the Lord before going into battle was a major factor in the initial defeat at Ai, and now the prayerlessness of Israel's leaders was about to precipitate another crisis.

The people had just returned to camp at Gilgal after hearing the Word of God read to them from Mt. Ebal and Mt. Gerizim. They had affirmed their willingness to obey God's Word. It was a time of spiritual victory, of euphoria, of elation—and thus it was also a made-to-order opportunity for satanic attack! God's people are never more vulnerable to the enemy's assault than when they think they have it made.

The Alliance with the Gibeonites (9:1–27)

Israel's victories over Jericho and Ai roused surrounding nations to concerted action. The frightened kings were grouped in three geographical areas: the hill country of central Palestine, the valleys or lowlands, and the coastal plain stretching north to Lebanon. That they were not able to unite into one fighting force as they wanted is a tribute to the success of Joshua's strategy of driving a wedge through the backbone of Canaan.

But powerful confederations were successfully formed in both the north and the south. Ancient tribal enemies declared truces in their wars, making a common-cause alliance against the invasion force of God's people.

When righteousness becomes aggressive and bent on an objective, it has a way of uniting both the forces of righteousness and the enemies of righteousness. It happened this way when Jesus launched his earthly ministry. His aggressive ministry of healing, preaching, and the confrontation of sin galvanized his own followers—but it also welded together three groups which had formerly been enemies, the Pharisees, the Sadducees, and the Herodians. Scripture predicts that His future return will have a similar effect. (See Ps. 2:2; Rev. 19:19.)

The more boldly the Christian faith advances, the more vocal and violent the opposition will become.

1. The Deception of the Gibeonites (9:3:15)

Despite the alliances being formed in the north and south, not all of Israel's enemies wanted to fight. Located in the hill country only six miles northwest of Jerusalem,

Gibeon was the leading city of a four-city republic. The Gibeonites were convinced that they could never defeat Israel in war, so they decided to "wage peace" instead.

After taking counsel among their leaders, the Gibeonites adopted an ingenious plan to send emissaries to Joshua, disguised as weary and worn travelers who had been on a long journey. When this deceitful delegation arrived in Gilgal, with their dirty garments, their dried and moldy food, their patched and parched wineskins, and their thin sandals, they went to Joshua with the message, "We have come from a far country; now, therefore, make a covenant with us."

Why did they place emphasis on being from a far country? Why did they go to such elaborate pains to create an image of themselves as travelers from afar? Apparently, the Gibeonites were aware of the provisions in the Mosaic Law permitting Israel to make peace with distant cities but requiring Israel to completely destroy the nearby cities of Canaan. (See Deut. 20:10–15.)

At first Joshua and his generals were hesitant. "Perhaps you are living within our land," Joshua responded warily. "How then shall we make a covenant with you?" It was well for them to be on their guard, for things are not always as they seem. Evil men are known to take advantage of the righteous. We, too, must always be on the alert, lest we fall prey to wolves masquerading in sheep's clothing.

Jesus warned His disciples, "Behold, I send you out as sheep in the midst of wolves; therefore be shrewd as serpents, and innocent as doves."[1] And the apostle Paul noted that "wolves" could come from anywhere—even appearing as part of the flock of God: "I know that after my departure savage wolves will come in among you, not sparing the flock; and from among your own selves men will arise, speaking perverse things, to draw away the disciples after themselves."[2] Christians should always be on guard against "wolves"—both those who would attack us from the outside and those who would undermine and spiritually seduce us from within the church.

As Joshua questioned them, the sly and underhanded Gibeonites told their tale. They insisted they came from a great distance to show respect to the powerful God of the Israelites. They claimed to want only to live at peace as Israel's servants. It is interesting that, in this dialogue, the Gibeonites make no reference to Israel's recent victories over Jericho and Ai—and perhaps this was part of their effort to appear to be what they were not: travelers from afar. People from a far country would be less likely to have heard of these recent battles.

Then the Gibeonites presented their credentials: the moldy bread, the patched wineskins, the ragged clothes. This ruse was successful: Joshua and the other leaders of Israel were fooled into dropping their guard. The cunning strategy of the Gibeonites worked, and the leaders of Israel concluded a formal treaty with them.

Joshua and the Israelite leaders made at least two major mistakes. First, they trusted evidence that was highly questionable. Envoys with power to conclude treaties with other nations should have substantial credentials. It was foolish of Joshua not to demand such credentials.

Many today are just as gullible, accepting dubious declarations as if they are scientific fact. As Dr. Carl Armerding observes, "When we hear some supposedly learned man talk about the skeletal remains of prehistoric man whose age runs into hundreds of thousands of years, one wonders if this is not some more of the devil's moldy bread."[3]

But what Christian is there who has not been similarly taken in by some of Satan's "moldy bread"? If we think we are smart enough to outfox Satan by our own strength and intellect, then we have seriously underestimated our enemy. As Paul exhorts us, "Put on the full armor of God, that you may be able to stand firm against the schemes of the devil."[4] We need to know that the enemy not only attacks us with a bold, full-frontal assault, but also by means of stealth and camouflage. (See and compare 1 Peter 5:8 and 2 Cor. 11:14.) Satan disguises himself to deceive men about themselves, about the purpose of life, about eternity. As F. B. Meyer notes,

> It is in this way that we are tempted still—more by the wiles of Satan than by his open assaults; more by the deceitfulness of sin than by its declared war. And it is little matter for wonder that those who succeed at Jericho and Ai fall into the nets woven and laid down by the wiles of Gibeon.[5]

The second and primary reason for Israel's failure is that the nation's leaders did not seek direction from God. They did not pray. They did not ask the high priests for guidance. They did not consult with their Commander-in-Chief.

A veteran missionary was once described with these words: "Throughout his life, his first step was always to pray; it was never his last resort." If only these words would have described Joshua and the nation of Israel at this crucial moment in their history.

Why did they enter into this contract without consulting God? Did Joshua and his men think the evidence of the Gibeonites was so far beyond question that they needed no counsel from Jehovah? Did they consider the matter too routine and unimportant to bother God about?

Whatever their reasons, it was a serious misjudgment for the leaders of Israel to make such a decision while leaving God out of their plans. It is an equally serious mistake when you and I do the same thing today. As F. B. Meyer adds,

> Before entering into any alliance—taking a partner in life, going into business with another, yielding assent to any proposition which involves confederation with others—be sure to ask counsel at the mouth of the Lord. He will assuredly answer by an irresistible impulse—by the voice of a friend; by a circumstance strange and unexpected; by a passage of Scripture. He will choose His own messenger; but He will send a message.[6]

2. Discovery of the Ruse (9:16–17)

A preacher once announced to his congregation that he would speak the following Sunday on the subject of lying. He requested that his audience prepare by reading Mark 17 during the week. The following Sunday, he asked how many had read the passage. About twenty hands shot up. The preacher leaned out over the edge of his pulpit and thundered, *"You're* the ones I'm preaching to this morning! There *isn't* any Mark 17!"

Lies can't stay covered up forever. Within a few days after concluding their treaty with the Gibeonites, Joshua and the leaders of Israel learned that they had been lied to and tricked. The Gibeonites lived in Canaan proper, about 20 miles from Gilgal, and not in some far country. An exploratory force confirmed the fraud by discovering the nearby location of Gibeon and its three dependent cities.

This account confirms the proverb: "A lying tongue is only for a moment."[7] Sooner or later, trickery and deceit are exposed and truth will out. Almost every day, our newspapers print yet another story which validates this principle: People cannot cover up their evil acts and schemes indefinitely. In the long run, lies will be exposed.

3. Decision of the Leaders (9:18–27)

When they discovered they had been duped, the Israelites wanted to disregard the covenant and destroy the Gibeonites. But Joshua and his generals declared that the deception did not nullify the treaty. The agreement was sacred because it had been ratified in the name of the Lord God of Israel. To break it would bring down the wrath of God on Israel. In fact, such a judgment from God would later come to pass during David's reign because Saul disregarded this agreement. (See 2 Sam. 21:1–6.)

Joshua and his fellow leaders were men of integrity who stood by their word. Though humiliated, they did not want to bring further disgrace upon God and His people by breaking a sacred treaty. It has been said that Joshua and his generals were more careful about their testimony than some Christians today.

Yet, though Israel would not go back on its pledge, the deceivers had to be punished. Joshua addressed the Gibeonites, rebuking them for their dishonesty and sentencing them to perpetual slavery. As slaves, the Gibeonites would become woodcutters and water-bearers for the Israelites. And to keep the Gibeonites' idolatry from defiling the true faith of Israel, their work would be carried out in the tabernacle, where they would be exposed to the worship of the one true God.

As a result, the very thing the Gibeonites hoped to retain—their freedom—was lost. But the curse eventually became a blessing. It was on behalf of the Gibeonites that God later worked a great miracle. (See Josh. 10:10–14.) Later, the tabernacle of the Lord would be pitched at Gibeon (see 2 Chron. 1:3), and the Gibeonites (later known as Nethinims) would replace the Levites in temple service (see Ezra 2:43 and 8:20).

That is the amazing way the grace of God works. He is still able to turn a curse into a blessing. While it is true that the natural consequences of our sin generally have to run their course, God in His grace not only forgives but in many cases He actually overrules our mistakes and brings blessing out of our sin.

Have you hastily and unwisely entered into an alliance with a modern-day Gibeonite? Are you now regretting some action you have taken out of haste, carelessness, or prayerlessness? Then seek God's forgiveness and grace. He is the only one who can bring triumph out of our tragedy, and joy out of our sorrow.

Defense of the Gibeonites (10:1–43)

Chapter 10 presents an interesting situation which reveals still more depth to the character of Joshua. The Gibeonites, who had just deceived the Israelites, then came under attack by an alliance of Amorite kings from southern Canaan. The Gibeonites urgently appealed to Israel for help—and from a purely human standpoint, Joshua would have been justified in saying, "Good riddance! Those lying Gibeonites are getting just what they deserve!" But Joshua did not do that. This chapter presents Joshua as a man of absolute honor and fidelity to his word.

In this account, we find another profound "secret" of godly leadership in the example of Joshua: *A true Christian leader keeps commitments.* "O Lord, who may abide in Thy tent?" asks the psalmist. "Who may dwell on Thy holy hill? He who walks with integrity, and works righteousness, and speaks truth in his heart. . . . He [who] swears to his own hurt, and does not change."[8] God honors us when we honor our commitments—even commitments we have entered into foolishly or which we have been tricked into, and even commitments which are costly to us. God honors the Christian leader who is reliable and dependable, and whose word can be trusted.

Last chapter, we saw that there is a clear dividing line between Joshua 7 and Joshua 8, and that a number of contrasts could be observed between those two chapters. Here, at the division point between chapters 9 and 10 we see a similar set of contrasts:

Chapter 9	**Chapter 10**
Israel is deceived by the Gibeonites	Israel defends the Gibeonites
Israel makes a treaty	Israel honors its treaty
Israel experiences peace	Israel engages in war

The structure of Joshua 10 can be broken down into three parts:

1. The Cause of the Conflict (10:1–5)
2. The Course of the Conflict (10:6–15)
3. The Culmination of the Conflict (10:16–43)

Let's examine each section in turn.

1. The Cause of the Conflict (10:1–5)

In those days, before becoming the capital of Jewish society, the city of Jerusalem was in the hands of the Amorites. Located just five miles south of Gibeon, Jerusalem had reason to be concerned about the plans and plottings of the Gibeonites. Upon learning that the Gibeonites had concluded a treated with the Israelite invaders, the destroyers of Jericho and Ai, Adoni-zedek, the king of Jerusalem, was seized with panic—and with good reason. The treacherous surrender of the Gibeonite cities completed an arc beginning at Gilgal and extending through Jericho and Ai to a point just a few miles northwest of Jerusalem. The handwriting was on the wall—Jersualem's security was severely threatened. If the advances of Israel's armies continued without challenge, Jerusalem would soon be surrounded and captured by the Israelites.

The king of Jerusalem sent an urgent message therefore to four other kings of southern Canaan, stressing the fact that Gibeon had made peace with Israel. This was a traitorous and punishable act, which could pave the way for other cities to surrender in like manner. It was a signal for the kings to take immediate action against Gibeon, and they wasted no time in forming an alliance to lay siege to Gibeon.

2. The Course of the Conflict (10:6–15)

Faced with certain slaughter, the Gibeonites sent a runner to Gilgal with an insistent appeal: "Come up to us quickly and save us and help us, for all the kings of the Amorites that live in the hill country have assembled against us."

The Israelites could have ignored the Gibeonites' pleas, thereby ridding themselves of a reminder of embarrassing failure. But that was not Joshua's style. It was not even an option as far as he was concerned. Joshua had made a treaty with the Gibeonites, and his integrity would not permit him to unilaterally abrogate it.

As often happens, there turned out to be a distinct advantage in maintaining integrity and keeping faith. In Joshua's case, it was a *military* advantage. Up to this time, Israel's army had attacked one fortified city at a time, which meant that Israel looked forward to a long and drawn-out offensive campaign for conquering the entire land of Canaan. But now Joshua had the strategic opening he needed to break the back of the enemy forces throughout the region: the combined Amorite armies of southern Canaan were exposed, camped in an open field outside Gibeon.

Gathering his forces, Joshua and his men marched the twenty-five miles from Gilgal to Gibeon under cover of darkness. From a human perspective, this long forced march was a risky, dangerous move on Joshua's part. It was an arduous and rugged journey, requiring an ascent of 4,000 feet over steep and difficult terrain. There was no opportunity for rest. By the time the Israelite army arrived at Gibeon, they were fatigued. A powerful foe was arrayed against them. If God did not intervene, all would be lost.

From a divine perspective, however, the outcome of the battle was assured. In verse 8, God promised Joshua, "Do not fear them, for I have given them into your hands; not one of them shall stand before you." Buoyed and uplifted by God's promise of victory, Joshua led a surprise attack on the Amorite armies of the south, possibly while it was still dark.

As the attacking Israelites fell upon them, the Amorites were seized with panic. After a short stand in which many were killed, they broke and fled in confusion toward the west. Their escape route led through a narrow pass and down the Valley of Aijalon, with the Israelites in hot pursuit. This great high-road which led down from the central hill country has frequently been the scene of rout and retreat, as in A.D. 66 when the Roman general Cestius Gallus fled by that road from Jewish rebel forces.

Unlike the Romans who followed that path 1,500 years later, the Amorites did not escape. Using the forces of nature to fight for Israel, the Lord brought down a storm of large hailstones. They fell on the enemy with such deadly precision that more Amorites died under the hailstones than by the edge of the sword.

This entire passage provides a striking illustration of the interplay between the human and divine factors which God uses to accomplish His purposes and bring about His victories. As you read the narrative, you see that it alternates between Joshua and Jehovah, between the human and the divine. The part that each played in this conflict is clearly defined. The people were commanded to fight, but God gave the victory.

Certainly, there are times when we can do nothing but wait for God to act. But overwhelmingly, we are to act in partnership with God, taking our commands from Him, living in dependence on his strength, confidently expecting him to keep His promises and do His part. God stands ready to act for us—but He is more interested in our character than our comfort. He knows that we cannot develop character by just sitting back and letting God do all the work. The Lord will not squander divine power in order to do miracles for us when we can achieve the same results with some human sweat and toil.

As the day of the Battle of Beth-horon wore on, Joshua knew that the pursuit of the enemy would be long and arduous. At the most, the military leader had twelve hours of daylight remaining. He clearly needed much more if he was to realize the fulfillment of God's promise and see the total annihilation of his foes. So Joshua brought a totally unprecedented request to God: "O Sun, stand still at Gibeon, and O Moon in the valley of Aijalon."

It was noon and the hot sun was directly overhead when Joshua uttered this prayer. The moon was on the horizon to the west. Joshua's petition, verse 13 tells us, was quickly answered: "So the sun stood still, and the moon stopped, until the nation [of Israel] avenged themselves of their enemies."

The record of this miracle has been considered a striking example of the supposed contradictions between Scripture and science. As we know, the sun does not move around the earth. Rather, the alternation of light and dark, of day and night, occurs because the earth rotates on its axis in relation to the sun. In addressing the sun rather than the earth, Joshua was simply using the language of observation. He was speaking from the perspective and appearance of things on earth. People still speak the same way, even in the scientific community. Scientists still record the hours of "sunrise" and "sunset," yet they are not accused of scientific error.

Joshua's long day, however, must be explained. As verse 14 says, "There was no day like that before it or after it." What actually did happen on that strange day? The possible answers are numerous. In fact, a research paper written by one seminarian discussed twelve explanations, and stated that these were only a few representative samples!

The explanation which does the most justice to the text is that, in answer to Joshua's prayer, God caused the rotation of the earth to *slow down* so that it made one full rotation in forty-eight hours rather than twenty-four. This makes much more sense than if the earth had stopped dead in its tracks!

The earth rotates at a rate of approximately one rotation every twenty-four hours, which means that a person standing at the equator is circling the earth's axis at a speed of *1035.4 miles an hour!* What would happen to that person if the earth's rotation suddenly ground to a halt? He would keep right on going! Clearly, if the earth simply *stopped*, the result would have been a worldwide cataclysm. Everything that wasn't nailed down (including Joshua and his army!) would have been thrown into space. Earthquakes and monstrous tidal waves would have pounded and shaken the planet. Since these dire cataclysms are not observed, then we must assume that, the earth's rotation did not stop.

A more likely explanation is that the earth's rotation *slowed*. Support for this explanation is found in verse 13: "And so the sun stopped in the middle of the sky, *and did not hasten to go down for about a whole day.*" The sun was thus abnormally slow in setting. From noon to dusk, it crept slowly and lethargically across the sky.

On May 7, 1973, *The Dallas Morning News* reported, "A giant storm on the sun last year probably slowed down the spinning of the earth for one rather long day." According to two scientists, this happened on August 4, 1972. "The length of day on any planet," the article concluded, "is governed by the time it takes to complete one full rotation. The faster it rotates, the shorter the day. So the earth must have slowed down fractionally."

In Joshua's time, just such a thing must have happened, so that this one remarkable day was extended by an additional twenty-four hours—all the time Joshua and his soldiers needed to complete their victorious battle.

An important fact that should not be overlooked is that the sun and moon were principal deities among the Canaanites. It may have seemed to the Canaanites that their gods were compelled to obey when the leader of the Israelites prayed to his God.

The secret of Israel's triumph over the coalition of Canaanites is found in the words of verse 14, "the Lord fought for Israel." In answer to prayer, Israel experienced the dramatic intervention of God, and victory was assured.

While Joshua's prolonged day was a miraculous event not to be repeated, God still listens when people call on him. He still responds to the cry of need and He intervenes on behalf of His children.

Just before World War II ended in Europe, a young soldier named Joel wrote to his mother in New Jersey, and told this story:

> One of my best buddies, Tom, with his whole platoon was pinned down by German mortar and artillery fire. They were given the order to move, but couldn't because the Germans had full view of them from a hill and were zeroing their fire in on them perfectly.
>
> Tom is the most conscientious Christian boy I have ever met in the service. He knew something had to be done to save the fifty men. He crawled from his foxhole and looked things over. Seeing how things were, he lay down behind a tree and earnestly prayed God to help them out of this situation. . . .
>
> After he prayed, a fog or mist rolled down between the two hills and the whole platoon got out of their foxholes and escaped. They reorganized in a little town behind the lines where there was a church building. They all went in and knelt down to pray and thank the Lord. Then they asked the kid to take the service.
>
> That is true, Ma, and it just shows how much prayer can mean—if that wasn't an answer to prayer, I don't know what is. You can bet that Tom is respected by his buddies.[9]

3. The Culmination of the Conflict (10:16–43)

Taking every advantage of the extended day, Joshua continued in hot pursuit of the enemy. The five strong kings and their armies had left their fortified cities to fight Israel in the open, and now Joshua was determined to prevent their return behind those walls. When word came that the kings had hidden in a cave, Joshua did not stop to deal with them but vigorously pursued the Amorite soldiers, killing all who did not escape to fortified cities. Then, returning to the guarded cave, he brought out the captured kings.

Following an ancient Eastern custom, often pictured on Egyptian and Assyrian monuments, Joshua instructed his field commanders to put their feet on the necks of the defeated kings. This was a symbol of the complete subjugation of the defeated enemy and a token of victories to come in the land of Canaan. "For thus the Lord will do to all your enemies with whom you fight," said Joshua, driving the symbolic message home to the hearts of his people. After the kings were killed, their bodies were exposed by hanging until sundown, when they were thrown into the cave which was then blocked by great stones. Thus we have another memorial of Israel's victorious march through Canaan.

People Who Know Their God

Most of us learn, early in our Christian experience, that we do not just face one enemy. We face a coalition of evil forces that have banded together in an attempt to destroy us. Those enemies are commonly called "the world," "the flesh," and "the devil." The world pressures us and hammers us and tries to conform us to its mold. The flesh is the sinfulness within us which betrays us and undermines us and sabotages us, even though we want to serve God with our minds and our bodies. The devil is the master strategist of the assault against us and sometimes attacks us openly, sometimes craftily, but always with an unerring sense of where our weaknesses lie.

Together, the world, the flesh, and the devil make an unbeatable combination—or they would be unbeatable, if not for the saving intervention of God. Without God, victory against such an alliance is impossible. With God, victory is assured!

A notorious alcoholic named Charlie was converted during the Welsh revival, and he immediately straightened out his life and became a sober and respectable man. But the tavern-keeper was disturbed over losing such a good (and profitable) patron as Charlie. One day the tavern-keeper was sweeping up in front of his place when he saw Charlie walking by. "Say, Charlie!" called the barkeep. "What's wrong, man? Why don't you come by anymore? You keep passing by this place, but you never come in anymore!"

Charlie paused and, with a heavenward glance, replied, "It's not that *I* keep going past," he said. "*We* go past, Him and I."

Charlie knew the secret of victory: The Lord is with us. He fights for us. As Paul said, "If God is for us, who can be against us?"[10]

The defeat of the five kings and their armies sealed the doom of southern Canaan. In a series of lightning-like raids, Joshua attacked the key military centers of the region in order to destroy any further military capability. First, Joshua took Makkedah, Libnah, Lachish, and Eglon. These cities, ranging roughly from north to south, guarded the approaches to the southern highlands. (Later, both Sennacherib and Nebuchadnezzar would follow the same strategy in their attacks on Judah.) Joshua next drove into the heart of the southern region and defeated its two walled cities, Hebron and Debir.

But Jerusalem, one of the five confederates, was bypassed. The troops may have been too weary to undertake this difficult task as they returned to camp at Gilgal. At any rate, for many years Jerusalem remained an island of paganism within an Israelite sea. The city would continue to be troublesome to the tribes of Judah and Benjamin until it was conquered by David. (See 2 Sam. 5:7.)

After a geographic summary of the extent of Israel's campaign in the south, the writer of the book of Joshua concludes with a statement (verse 42) that gives credibility to the impressive sweep of victories recorded in this chapter: "And Joshua captured all these kings and their lands at one time, because the Lord, the God of Israel, fought for Israel." It is with this supreme confidence in God that Joshua and his tired armies returned to Gilgal to make preparations for the completion of their task.

When Mark Twain was traveling in Europe with his young daughter, he was honored and toasted in city after city by royalty and by celebrities in the arts and sciences. Toward the end of their journey, his daughter remarked to him, "Papa, you know everybody but God, don't you?"

Joshua was a man who knew God above all else. The results are impressively recorded here. As Daniel later wrote, "The people who know their God will display strength and take action."[11] For Joshua, for Daniel, and for you and me, the key to victory is knowing God personally and trusting Him completely.

QUESTIONS FOR REFLECTION AND DISCUSSION

See Your Own Reflection

1. If you found out that tomorrow was going to be a unique, once-in-a-lifetime forty-eight hour day, how would you spend it?

Dig a Little Deeper

2. Why were Joshua and his generals fooled by the Gibeonites?

How did Joshua respond to being tricked by the Gibeonites?

What was the Gibeonites' response to the sentence Joshua imposed on them?

3. Put yourself in the sandals of Joshua and his generals as the rag-tag delegation from Gibeon arrives, claiming to come from afar and seeking a peace treaty. Would you have been fooled? Why or why not?

Can you think of any parallel experiences in your own life when you were either fooled as Joshua was, or you saw through a deception and avoided a big blunder? Why do you think you were fooled/not fooled?

4. Can you think of some modern-day "Gibeonites" who try to deceive Christians into making unwise alliances with them? What kinds of agreements and alliances are we in danger of making? How can we guard against being deceived?

5. If you were Joshua, would you:

• Keep the treaty with the Gibeonites—or break it?

• Make the Gibeonites your slaves, kill them, or forgive them and let them go in peace?

• Go to war and help the Gibeonites—or let them be wiped out by the Amorites?

What do your answers to these questions say about you?

6. Joshua kept his word to the Gibeonites, even though he had been conned into giving his word in the first place. Do we, as Christians, need to keep our word in the following situations?

• You promised to let your son go on the Disneyland trip with his youth group if he brought that D in Algebra up to a C. He promised and he has led you to believe he has been doing well in class. The Disneyland trip is tomorrow. The money for the trip has all been paid. Your son is looking forward to it. But your son's math teacher has just called to tell you that your son's D has dropped to an F. What do you do?

• You are on the church board. Your pastor urged you to take the chairmanship of the stewardship committee, even though you felt it was more than you could handle. He promised you that he would work closely with you, to be at every meeting with you, and to meet with you once a week for prayer and strategy sessions. Now that you are in the job, you find that your pastor has not kept any of his promises. You are not just overwhelmed, you are *drowning in* the job. You want to resign, but you promised to give the job a full year. What should you do?

• As a commercial landlord, you have just signed a two-year lease with a couple who want to open a "family bookstore." Now you find out that the so-called "family bookstore" sells nothing but hard-core pornography. The zoning law allows them to operate an X-rated bookstore at that location. Nothing in the lease forbids them to operate that kind of business on your property. There's no law against lying to the landlord. But you have been tricked—and now that property is going to be used in a way that completely violates your beliefs and values. What should you do?

Let's Get Personal

7. If you had seen the miracle of the sun seeming to stand still, how would you have felt? Would it make you so certain of the reality of God that you would no longer need faith? Would it make you confident that God cares for you? Would it make you afraid of God's incomprehen-

sible power? In your own life, do you seek after miracles—or avoid them?

8. Is there anyone in your life that you could call on for help if you were being "attacked by the Amorites"?

If not, why not? Is it because no one has reached out to you? Or is it because you have not reached out to anyone else?

8

VANQUISHING ENEMIES

JOSHUA 11–12

Near the end of his illustrious career, Sir Winston Churchill was invited back to his preparatory school to address the young men. Before Sir Winston arrived, the headmaster said to the students, "The prime minister will soon be here. Since he is one of the greatest men of all time, I challenge you all to listen carefully and take notes on what Sir Winston has to say."

Churchill arrived and was duly given an effusive introduction, after which he stepped up to the lectern and began to speak. Here is the complete text of his address:

Young gentlemen, never give up. Never give up. Never, never, never, never!

Then he sat down. The entire lecture had been given—probably the shortest speech in history. But who in that audience would ever forget Churchill's words?

Never give up!
Perseverance!
Persistence!
Relentless pursuit of the goal!

That is the stuff victories are made of—both in the life of Churchill, the man who guided England through its "darkest hour" in World War II, and in the life of Joshua, who charted the course of Israel through some of its most perilous days. Joshua was a man who personified persistence. Relentlessly, tirelessly, he pursued the goal of vanquishing the Canaanites and possessing the land of promise. After the long, exhausting military campaign in the south, he did not enjoy any prolonged period of recuperation before facing an even stiffer challenge: the massive coalition of Canaanite forces in the north.

But thanks to his tireless persistence, Joshua was equal to the task. As Charles Swindoll writes,

> How many military battles would never have been won without persistence? How many men and women would never have graduated from school . . . or changed careers in midstream . . . or stayed together in marriage . . . or reared a retarded child? Think of the criminal cases that would never have been solved without the relentless persistence of detectives. How about the great music that would never have been finished, the grand pieces of art that would never have graced museums, cathedrals, and monuments the world over? Back behind the impeccable beauty of each work is a dream that wouldn't die mixed with the dogged determination of a genius of whom this indifferent world is not worthy. . . .
>
> I heard about a couple of men who were working alongside the inventor Thomas Edison. Weary to the point of exasperation, one man sighed, "What a waste! We have tried no less than seven hundred experiments and *nothing* has worked. We are not a bit better off than when we started."
>
> With an optimistic twinkle in his eye, Edison quipped, "Oh, yes, we are! We now know seven hundred things that *won't* work. We're closer than we've

ever been before." With that, he rolled up his sleeves and plunged back in.[1]

A Military Genius, a Spiritual Giant

Stuart Briscoe has said that the three qualifications for a Christian leader are "the mind of a scholar, the heart of a child, and the hide of a rhinoceros." Israel's leader was that kind of man. He had a keen, trained mind, steeped in the knowledge of the Word of God and the history of his people. He had a childlike heart which not only believed in God but matter-of-factly *expected* to see God act. He had the rhino's hide necessary for a man of war, a man who stood in the bloody crossroads of history, a man who had to make tough decisions. The fate of a nation and of many individual lives depended on his decisions, but he made them boldly and courageously. He was a leader.

Joshua was both a military genius and a spiritual giant. As a military leader, he was nothing short of brilliant. He never fought a defensive war; he was always on the offensive, always keeping the enemy off balance, always driving forward. He was an expert at feints and decoy maneuvers. He never failed to exploit an unexpected opportunity, such as the opportunity which presented itself when the kings of the south gathered against the Gibeonites. He was a master tactician, the "Stormin' Norman" Schwarzkopf of his era.

As a spiritual leader, however, he was equally exemplary. He was a model of faith and godly character to his people. He stood by the promise made to Rahab by the spies. He kept faith with the deceiving Gibeonites. He refused to use his great position for personal gain.

With this great leader at the helm of Israel's affairs, the conquest of Canaan entered its final phase. Ahead lay total victory.

The Victory in the North (11:1–15)

An ill wind from the south brought terrifying news to the Canaanite kings of the north: Joshua's army was crushing all opposition and taking over the southern part of Canaan. Soon, Joshua would look to the north for more fields of conquest.

Jabin, king of Hazor, organized a last desperate attempt to stop the conquest of the land by the armies of Israel. No doubt his attempt would have had a better chance to succeed had he joined the coalition of Adonizedek, marching in force from the north to crush the army of Israel in a giant claw. But God restrained Jabin from such a move until the problem had festered into a crisis. Now, as Jabin made his move, it was a move born of panic and desperation.

One of Jabin's biggest mistakes was *haste*.

1. The Confederation (11:1–5)

Messengers fanned out rapidly in all directions— north, south, east, and west—with an urgent call to arms. It may have been quite similar to the summons Saul issued later for Israel to follow him to Jabesh-Gilead. Saul killed a yoke of oxen and sent pieces of the animals by couriers who cried, "Whoever does not come out after Saul and after Samuel, so shall it be done to his oxen." (See 1 Sam. 11:7.)

Although there was no love lost between these kings of the north, the threat of annihilation forced them into an alliance. They joined forces a few miles northwest of the Sea of Galilee in a plain near the waters of Merom.

The combined army was impressive. Not only did it include soldiers in number "as the sand that is on the seashore," but it also boasted horses and chariots in great numbers. Josephus, the Jewish historian who lived in the first century A.D., speculated that this northern confederacy included 300,000 infantry soldiers, 10,000 cavalry troops, and 20,000 chariots.

The odds against the Israelites seemed overwhelming. How could Joshua hope to win this battle?

The Conflict (11:6–15)

The vast host of Canaanites were pitched at the waters of Merom. It was probably their plan to sweep down the Jordan Valley and attack Joshua at Gilgal. But Joshua did not wait for the battle to come to him. He was already marching toward Merom, a five-day trek from his home base. As he marched, he had a lot of time to think about the immense host of Canaanite soldiers arrayed against him. The prospect of such a battle would give any military commander pause.

But God spoke to Joshua's heart, and the words He spoke were words of promise and encouragement, clear and bracing: "Do not be afraid because of them, for tomorrow at this time I will deliver all of them slain before Israel." The promise was clear, definite, concrete—just like the promises God has made to us in His Word. This message was just what Joshua needed, and the leader of Israel took this promise at face value. He believed that God would give him a victory over what might well turn out to be Israel's greatest foe.

The battle took place in two phases. The next day, Joshua surprised the enemy, attacking them at the waters of Merom and chasing them westward to the coast (to Sidon and Misrephoth-maim), and eastward to the valley of Mizpeh. Following God's directions to the letter, Joshua killed all of the enemy, burned the chariots, and lamed the horses.

But why did God command such drastic actions as

burning the chariots and hamstringing the horses? Because the Canaanites used horses in their pagan worship. Also there was the danger that Israel might trust in these new weapons of war rather than in the Lord. As the psalmist declared, "Some boast in chariots, and some in horses; but we will boast in the name of the Lord, our God."[2]

Perhaps the horses and chariots might have been to Israel what nuclear power is to our own nation. Can superior nuclear weaponry be an absolute guarantee of security? Do we feel safer at night, knowing that the world is "guarded" by nuclear weapons—weapons that are not only in U.S. or British or French hands, but in the hands of the Chinese, the Ukranians, the North Koreans, and the Iraqis? Do we really live by what we declare on our coinage: IN GOD WE TRUST? Or do we place our trust in nuclear warheads, M-1 tanks, and Patriot missiles?

In the second phase of the war for northern Canaan, Joshua returned after routing the enemy army and capturing all the cities of the defeated kings. The city of Hazor, however, was singled out for special treatment, probably because it was by far the largest city in ancient Palestine. Hazor was fourteen times larger than Megiddo, and twenty-five times larger than Jericho. Occupying a position of immense strategic importance, Hazor dominated several branches of an ancient highway leading from Egypt to Syria, and on to Assyria and Babylon. Hazor alone among the norther cities was both seized and burned.

While Joshua may have decided to save the other captured cities for later Israelite use, he was determined to make a lasting example of Hazor, capital of all those city-states and the convener of their armies. If great Hazor could not escape, the Canaanites would be forced to acknowledge that any city could be burned if Joshua so decreed.

Thus a decisive victory was won in the north. And the key was *obedience to God.* "Just as the Lord had commanded Moses His servant, so Moses commanded Joshua, and so Joshua did; he left nothing undone of all that the Lord had commanded Moses."

Marshal Foch, in the second battle of the Marne during World War I, was asked about his situation. He sent back this dispatch. "My left falters. My center is weak. My right crumbles. I am attacking." Joshua, too, was always attacking, because those were his orders.

But those orders also included the total extermination of the Canaanite people of the land—an extreme measure which has caused some to reject this so-called "notorious book of Joshua" and to characterize the God who ordered such barbaric-seeming acts as "a Holy Terror."

In response to such reactions it needs to be reaffirmed that responsibility for the destruction of the Canaanites does not rest with Joshua and the Israelites, but with their divine Commander-in-Chief, Jehovah Himself. Israel simply carried out the orders of God. (See Deut. 20:16–17.)

Let sinful people and nations take note: God does not countenance sin indefinitely. History clearly attests to this fact. Nations, as well as individuals, can be guilty of sin. The bloody, vice-ridden, degenerate societies of the past—Assyria, Babylon, Greece, Rome—have all fallen, consumed as much from within as from without, victims of their own foolishness and sin. The death of the Third Reich was as much a divine judgment as it was a military defeat; that brutal, hate-filled Nazi state, with its systematic extermination of the Jews, richly deserved its destruction. Moreover, it is clear to see that many of the ills America continues to suffer in the 1990s are a direct, straight-line result of the obscene practice of slavery, which was once officially tolerated on our shores.

In 1863, Abraham Lincoln issued the following proclamation:

> We have been the recipients of the choicest bounties of heaven. We have been preserved, these many years, in peace and prosperity. We have grown in numbers, wealth, and power as no other nation has ever grown, but we have forgotten God. We have forgotten the gracious hand which preserved us in peace, and multiplied and enriched and strengthened us. And we have vainly imagined, in the deceitfulness of our hearts, that all these blessings were produced by some superior wisdom and virtue of our own. Intoxicated by unbroken success, we have become too self-sufficient to feel the necessity of redeeming and preserving grace, too proud to pray to the God that made us: It behooves us, then, to humble ourselves before the offended Power, to confess our national sins, and to pray for clemency and forgiveness.

These are warnings which apply to America in the 1990s. And they are words we would do well to heed.

The Conquest Summarized (11:16–12:24)

Victory in the north brought about the formal end of the conquest. Before recording how the land was apportioned among the tribes, the author paused to review and summarize the scope of the triumph in Canaan. Included is a description of the conquered geographic areas (11:16–23) and a list of the defeated kings (12:1–24).

1. The Conquered Areas (11:16–23)

The battles fought by Joshua and his troops ranged over lands that stretched from border to border, from south to north and from east to west. The period of conquest lasted a long time, and victory did not come easily or quickly. Victory rarely does.

Yet, out of all these military confrontations, only Gibeon sought peace. The other cities were taken in battle, God having hardened their hearts to fight Israel so that they might be destroyed. The Canaanites' day of grace has passed; the day of judgment had come. They had sinned against the light of the revelation of God in nature, in conscience, and in His recent miraculous works at the Red Sea, the Jordan River, and Jericho. Before the judgment, the sovereign God confirmed the hearts of these unrepentant people in their stubborn unbelief.

Special mention is made of the Anakim, the giants who had terrified the spies forty years before. These are the people of whom it had been said, "Who can stand before the sons of Anak?" (See Deut. 9:2.) These supposedly invincible foes were utterly destroyed. None remained—except a few scattered remnants in the remote cities of Gaza, Gath, and Ashdod. This omission proved unfortunate for Israel's later history, however. In David's time, the giant Goliath came from Gath to trouble Israel and defy Israel's God.

This section concludes with a declaration which summarizes the entire book of Joshua: "So Joshua took the whole land, according to all that the Lord had spoken to Moses, and Joshua gave it for an inheritance to Israel, according to their division by their tribes. Thus the land had rest from war." This verse looks back to the conquest, in chapters 1–11, and forward to the distribution of the land, chapters 13–22.

But how are we to understand the statement that "Joshua took the whole land" when we read that "very much of the land remains to be possessed"? (See 13:1.) To the Hebrew mind, the part stands for the whole. It thus only needs to be demonstrated that Joshua took key centers in all parts of the land to validate the statement that he had conquered the whole land.

In an article in the *Concordia Theological Monthly*,[3] A. J. Mattill, Jr., carefully analyzed the conquest of Canaan by surveying the geographical divisions of the land and the strategic sites which Joshua had conquered in each region. Included were conquered sites on the coastal plain, the shephelah (foothills), the central plateau, the Jordan Valley, and the Transjordan plateau. No area was totally bypassed. Joshua did indeed take control of the whole land, just as God promised he would if he followed the divine Word rather than human wisdom. (See Josh. 1:8.)

Joshua's accomplishments are even more astounding, given the tremendous odds against him. What made these "impossible" accomplishments possible was that Joshua trusted in God. As Dr. Richard Halverson reminds us, the same faith that Joshua had is available to you and me as well:

> When the situation is hopeless . . . . *That's the time for faith!* Actually, there is *no such thing as a hopeless situation* for one who trusts in God. . . . But the fact is that most of us turn to God *only when we think the situation's hopeless.* As long as we can find something in our circumstances on which to pin our hope we trust that *possibility* rather than God. Until we *have used up all our options*—see no shred of hope in our circumstances. . . . Then—*as a last resort*—we may turn to God. Someone put it this way: "As long as we have reason for hope, we hope in reason." As long as we can think up possible answers—*we depend upon human ingenuity*—or luck—or coincidence—etc.

Then, when *alternatives are exhausted* and there is
nowhere else to turn . . . . We *give God His chance.*
How much better to *trust God no matter what!*[4]

Joshua trusted God no matter what. When he faced
the impossible, he simply waited to see what sort of miracle God would perform. He walked by faith and not by
sight.

2. The Conquered Kings (12:1–24)

Concluding the story begun in Joshua 1 is a detailed
catalog of the kings defeated by Israel. The preceding
chapters list the major battles. Only in Joshua 12 do we
find a complete list of the conquered kings. Israel did not
occupy all of these cities, for Joshua did not have sufficient
manpower to leave a controlling garrison in each place.
But the defensive strength of each city was broken. Joshua
no doubt reasoned that the actual occupation by the
respective tribes should not be too difficult to carry out.

Joshua 12:1–6 records the victories under Moses on
the east side of Jordan. (See Num. 21; Deut. 2:24–3:17.)
the defeated cities on the west side of the river are listed
in Joshua 12:7–24. In this section, the kings of southern
Canaan are listed first (verses 9–16), and then the kings
of northern Canaan (verses 17–24).

It is surprising to find 31 kings in a land that is only
150 miles from north to south, and 50 miles from east to
west—an area roughly the size of the state of Vermont!
The reason is that these kings were rulers over city-
states, and they had only local authority. Apart from the
confederations that were formed by the kings of Jerusalem and Hazor, the lack of central government in Canaan
made the task of conquest somewhat easier for Israel
than it might have been had all these city-states been
united under a single government.

Reflecting on the significance of Joshua's victories, Bible commentator Henry T. Sell notes, "There has never been a greater war for a greater cause. The battle of Waterloo decided the fate of Europe, but this series of contests in far-off Canaan decided the fate of the world."[5]

Many of us are tempted to look at Joshua and say, "Yes, there was a man who changed the fate of the world. Yes, Joshua was a great man of God. Wouldn't it be something to be like Joshua?" Well, why can't we be like Joshua? Why can't you and I aspire to be godly leaders, full of faith and determination like Joshua was? We may not be able to *change the fate* of the world—but we can *have an influence* on the world for God. We can change our little part of the world. And if enough Christians decide to pattern themselves on the leadership model of Joshua, think of the changes we could make in this world!

The "secret" of godly leadership that we find in Joshua chapters 11 and 12 is: *A true Christian leader is persistent. He perseveres to the end. He never gives up.* As Christian leaders, God calls us to relentlessly, tirelessly pursue the goals he has given us. He goes along with us, in us, and before us as we face our enemies—our sins and habits, our temptations, the wiles of Satan, the opposition of circumstances and of other people, the enemy of fatigue and depression—and he enables us to knock those enemies down, one by one by one.

So don't give up! Keep on going! God is giving you the victory! He has brought you into the land across the Jordan, and He will give you the strength you need to possess that land—if you will remain faithful and persistent. "And let us not lose heart in doing good," wrote the apostle Paul, "for in due time we shall reap if we do not grow weary."[6]

In his business best-seller *Swim with the Sharks Without Being Eaten Alive*, Harvey Mackay (the man *Fortune* magazine called "Mr. Make-Things-Happen") tells the story of a man who personifies persistence. That man's name: Jack Mackay, Harvey Mackay's father. As a reporter for the Associated Press, Jack Mackay covered a sensational 1933 murder trial in Minneapolis. A man named Leonard Hankins was accused of being a member of the Ma Barker-Alvin Karpis gang, and convicted of killing an innocent bystander during a $118,000 bank robbery. Hankins was sentenced to life in prison.

In 1935, after most of the Barker-Karpis gang were either dead or in prison, several members of the gang revealed that Hankins was not involved in the robbery, and was not even a member of the gang. So Jack Mackay began a one-man crusade to win Leonard Hankins' release. He persuaded Minnesota governor Floyd Olson to begin an investigation, but Olson died in office with nothing accomplished. In 1939, Mackay persuaded Olson's successor, Harold Stassen to investigate, and the Stassen report—issued two years later in 1941—cleared Hankins. But as Hankins was about to be released, a hold order was placed on him because Kentucky officials wanted him extradited to face charges for a $13 robbery in Paducah.

After holding a man in prison almost a decade for a crime he didn't commit, Minnesota authorities didn't want to ship him to a prison in Kentucky for a $13 crime—so, to circumvent the extradition laws, they placed him in a mental asylum! There he stayed for many years, as Mackay wrote numerous AP stories, visited Hankins in prison (he was Hankins' only visitor at Thanksgiving and Christmas), and tried numerous times to win Hankins' release. In 1949, Hankins was moved out of the asylum—but instead of being released, he was shipped back to prison!

In 1951, Mackay persuaded Governor C. Elmer Anderson to convene the pardon board to hear Hankins' case. After eighteen years—including ten years in a mental institution—Hankins was finally pardoned and set free for a crime he did not commit. Harvey Mackay sums up his father's spirit in seven words: "That was Jack Mackay. Determination and heart."7

Would you and I have the persistence and determination to take on the legal system for *eighteen years* to see that justice was done? Would we be willing to pursue *any* goal with that kind of single-minded purpose? Are we the kind of Christians who never give up—or do we throw in the towel when the going gets tough?

Would you be willing to pray persistently, every single day for eighteen years, for that son or daughter, that parent, that friend or neighbor, to come to know the Lord? Would you be willing to work for eighteen years to accomplish that goal, to achieve that position, to write that book, to build that church, to launch that business or that missionary enterprise? What would it take to stop you? What would it take to discourage you and defeat you?

Jack Mackay didn't give up. Joshua didn't give up. If you and I want to gain the victory and "possess the land," then we mustn't give up either. Whatever your endeavor, whatever your goal, the key to success is *persistence*.

Drawn Swords to the Gates of Heaven

In *Pilgrim's Progress*, John Bunyan describes how the Interpreter conducted the book's hero, Christian, to a place where he could see a stately, shining palace. On top of the palace, there were people walking, clothed in gold. Around the door stood a great company of people wanting to go into the palace, but who dared not enter. A little distance from the door, a scribe sat at a table with a book and inkhorn to take the name of any person who would enter the palace. And in the doorway stood fierce men in armor, who were resolved to cut down anyone attempting to enter.

As Christian watched, one man separated himself from the crowd of those who were afraid to enter the palace. This courageous man stepped up to the scribe with the inkhorn and said, "Set down my name, sir." The scribe did so. Then the courageous man put a helmet on his head, drew a sword, and rushed toward the armed men who barred the doorway. A horrible fight ensued, and the courageous man received many sword-wounds from the guards in the doorway. Finally, Christian observed that the man had succeeded in slashing and hacking his way into the palace. Wounded and bleeding, he had nevertheless achieved his goal.

Then, from the towers of the palace, Christian heard voices—the voices of the people clothed in gold. They sang to the man who had just entered the palace, "Come in, come in! Eternal glory thou shalt win!"

You know how that man feels. You feel right now that you are cutting your way through a solid wall of opposition. That is what life is like for the Christian leader. It is a case of "drawn swords to the very gates of heaven."

But victory is coming! We have set our feet in the footprints of Joshua. We have believed God. We have taken Him at His Word. We are trusting His promises and we are relying on His presence. With patience and persistence, we will soon see our enemies vanquished, and the "land of promise" will be ours.

"This is the victory that has overcome the world," says 1 John 5:4—"our faith."

QUESTIONS FOR REFLECTION AND DISCUSSION

See Your Own Reflection

1. If you were Joshua right now, which of the following statements would best describe your life—and *why?*

❏ "I'm up to my neck in enemies! Lord, what should I do?"

❏ "I'm taking the battle to my enemies! Fight for me, Lord!"

❏ "We're winning the battle—but I'm sure getting tired of fighting!"

❏ "The war is over, the land can rest—and so can I!"

Dig a Little Deeper

2. Examine 11:1–11. Why did God instruct Joshua to destroy even the horses and chariots? Wasn't that wasteful, when the Israelites could have put those animals and war-machines to use?

3. Why did God single out Hazor for especially fierce destruction?

4. Verses 1 through 6 list the kings and the lands which were conquered under Moses' leadership. Verses 7 through 24 list all the kings and lands conquered under Joshua's leadership. Admittedly, these lists don't exactly make fascinating reading for us today, but God places these lists in His Word for a reason. Why do you think these lists were important to the people of Israel?

5. Many of the scenes and events in these chapters are shocking to our New Testament sensibilities: the slaughter of whole populations, the burning and pillaging of cities, the public humiliation and execution of kings— all by the order of God! How do you reconcile the God of Joshua with the God of John, who wrote, "God is love" (1 John 4:8)?

6. How is the conquest and extermination of the Canaanites by Joshua's army any different from the conquest and extermination that Hitler waged against the Jews and other populations before and during World War II? Are the actions of the Israelites morally defensible—or are they war crimes?

Let's Get Personal

7. Does God *always* give us success if we are obedient to God? Why or why not?

8. Have you experienced victory over an enemy in some area of your life? What role did *persistence* and *perseverance* play in that victory?

In what area of your life are you still seeking to gain the victory by obedience, persistence, and faith in God?

9

THE DIVINE REALTOR
AT WORK

JOSHUA 13–17

One of the town's leading citizens was approaching his ninetieth birthday, so the local newspaper sent a reporter to interview the man. Said the interviewer, "To what do you attribute your advanced age?"

"Well, to lots of things," said the man. "But mostly to the fact that I haven't died yet."

At the beginning of Joshua 13, the Lord comes to Joshua and says, "You are old and advanced in years." Does anyone like to be reminded that old age has come (or even that it is on the way)? I don't. I suspect you don't either. But however much we may want to cling to our youth and our vigor, that time will inevitably come for us, just as it came for Joshua. He was old—but his work was not yet done.

Old age is a time when most people reflect on the times of their lives—on the things they have done or wish they had done, and on what their lives have meant in the larger view of things. In his advancing years, the eighteenth-century English sculptor, John Bacon, made out his will and asked that this inscription be carved on his grave marker:

> What I was as an artist
> seemed to me of some importance while I lived.
> What I really was as a believer in
> Christ Jesus is the only thing
> of importance to me now.

Another man, a faithful pastor, called his family to his sickbed when he sensed that death was near. "I'm ready to go," he told them. "I've had a good life. I'm thankful for my wonderful wife, for my children, and for the forty years of ministry God gave me. I didn't do anything you would call 'great,' the way most people measure greatness. But I touched a life here and there for God, and I did His will. That's what really counts."

Joshua, too, has done what really counts. He has been a good and faithful servant to his Lord. We don't see any sign of regret or pain when the Lord tells him that much of the work of possessing the land remains undone, and that he will not live to complete it all.

Certainly, Joshua still had work to do. He was not going to fade into oblivion. Rather, Joshua the soldier was about to give way to Joshua the administrator. The conquered land would now be assigned to the various tribes. Joshua himself would oversee this important real estate transaction. It would be a less exhausting service for him to perform, and one better suited to his advancing years.

In his role as a soldier and a general, Joshua was a visionary, an innovator, a motivator, an entrepreneur of war. But his new role would call for a different set of skills, a different style of leadership, and a different approach to dealing with people. Joshua had to become what today we call a "manager." In his book *People And Performance: The Best Of Peter Drucker On Management*, management expert Peter F. Drucker explains what the job of a manager entails:

First, says Drucker, a manager *sets objectives*; he sets the goals, decides what has to be done to meet the goals, and communicates these decisions to the people. Second, a manager *organizes*; he classifies the work, divides it into manageable tasks, and assigns it to those who will carry it out. Third, a manager *motivates and communicates*; he takes a group of people and organizes them into a team, focused on a clear purpose; he rewards and promotes and offers incentive. Fourth, a manager *measures performance*; he analyses, appraises, and interprets the accomplishments of the team. Fifth and finally, a good manager *develops people*; he directs them, trains them, inspires them, and strengthens them to be people of diligence, integrity, and character.[1] Throughout the remainder of our study in the life of Joshua, we will see how Joshua carries out these important functions as the manager-administrator of the nation of Israel.

As you enter this section of the book of Joshua, you may feel it is tedious reading, with its detailed lists of boundaries and cities. Someone suggested that most of this section reads like a real estate deed. And that is precisely what we have in these lengthy narrations: detailed legal descriptions of the areas allocated to the twelve tribes. Title deeds may not make for riveting drama, but they are critically important documents and should not be regarded as insignificant or superfluous.

We also need to remember that this was a climactic moment in the life of the young nation. After centuries in Egyptian bondage, decades in the barren wilderness, and years of hard fighting in Canaan, the hour had arrived when the Israelites could at last settle down to build homes, cultivate the soil, raise their families, and live in peace in their own land. The day of land allotment must have been a joyous day indeed!

The Divine Command to Divide the Land (13:1–7)

"Now therefore apportion the land for an inheritance to the nine tribes, and the half-tribe of Manasseh," said the Lord in verse 7. He thus directed Joshua to divide the land west of the Jordan.

Since Joshua died at the age of 110 (see 24:29), he was probably at least 100 by this time. And God's commission to Joshua had included not only the conquest of the land but also its distribution to the tribes. He therefore needed to move quickly to this new assignment.

The task of allocation would take place at once, even though there remained much land to possess. The unconquered lands are listed from south to north and include what we know as Philistia, Phoenicia, and Lebanon. God promised to drive out the inhabitants of these areas, and Joshua was to allot them now, even though they were still occupied by the enemy. The work of conquest begun under Joshua would be finished by someone else, so Joshua was now being recommissioned in an administrative role. Perhaps God also wanted to remind Joshua that this grand operation was not his, but God's. As William Blaikie observed,

> God is not limited to one instrument, or to one age, or to one plan. Never does Providence appear to us so strange as when a noble worker is cut down in the very midst of his work. A young missionary has just shown

his splendid capacity for service, when fever strikes him low, and in a few days all that remains of him is rotting in the ground.

"What can God mean?" we sometimes ask impatiently. "Does He not know the rare value and the extreme scarcity of such men, that He sets them up apparently just to throw them down?" . . . But He is not limited to single agents. When Stephen died, He raised up Saul. For Wycliffe He gave Luther. When George Wishart was burnt He raised up John Knox. . . . So Joshua must be content to have done his part, and done it well, although he did not conquer all the land, and there yet remained much to be possessed.[2]

The Special Grant to the Eastern Tribes (13:8–33)

Joshua was next called upon to recognize and confirm what had already been done by Moses on the east side of the Jordan. The tribes of Reuben, Gad, and the half-tribe of Manasseh possessed large herds of cattle, and were anxious to settle in the rich grazing lands of Transjordan—that is, the lands east of the Jordan. Only when these Transjordanian tribes accepted the challenge to go west of the Jordan and fight alongside their brothers to win Canaan did Moses agree to assign the lands east of the Jordan to these tribes.

Reuben received the territory previously occupied by Moab, east of the Dead Sea. Gad's inheritance, in the center of the region, was in the original land of Gilead. The allotment to the half-tribe of Manasseh was the rich tableland of Bashan, east of the Sea of Galilee.

There is an interesting historical background concerning Reuben's portion. Centuries before the land was divided, Jacob made several prophecies regarding his sons as he lay on his deathbed. Concerning Reuben, he said, "Reuben, you are my firstborn; my might, and the beginning of my strength, preeminent in dignity, and pre-eminent in power. Uncontrolled as water, you shall not have preeminence, because you went up to your father's bed; then you defiled it" (Gen. 49:3–4; see also Gen. 35:22). Though he was the firstborn and entitled to a double portion (Deut. 21:17), neither he nor his tribe received it, because of Reuben's act of sin with his father's concubine, Bilhah. More than three centuries after the deed, the punishment for Reuben's sin was passed on to his descendents. The right of the firstborn passed to his brother Joseph who received two portions, one for Ephraim and the other for Manasseh.

Was the request of the tribes of Reuben, Gad, and Manasseh to settle in Transjordan a wise one? History would seem to answer No. Their territories had no natu-ral boundaries to the east, and were constantly exposed to invasion by the Moabites, Canaanites, Syrians, Midi-anites, Amalekites, and others. And when the king of Assyria looked covetously toward Canaan, the two and one-half tribes were the first to be carried into captivity by the Assyrian armies. (See 1 Chron. 5:26.)

By contrast with the rich though dangerous inherit-ance of these tribes, the tribe of Levi received no inherit-ance from Moses. At first this might seem puzzling, but closer examination reveals that in lieu of territorial pos-sessions, the tribe of Levi was allotted the sacrifices or offerings (Josh. 13:14), the priesthood (18:7), and the Lord Himself (13:33). Who could dream of a greater inheritance?

The two and one-half tribes chose on the basis of appearances, just as Lot did when he chose to settle on the Plain of Sodom (Genesis 13). As a result, their inher-itance was ultimately lost to them. On the other hand, the

Levites—who requested no portion—were given an inheritance of abiding spiritual significance.

This reminds us of the words of Jesus, "Do not lay up for yourselves treasures upon earth, where moth and rust destroy, and where thieves break in and steal. But lay up for yourselves treasures in heaven, where neither moth nor rust destroys, and where thieves do not break in or steal; for where your treasure is, there will your heart be also."[3]

In the south of France, near the Mediterranean coast, you may still see an old tombstone inscribed with these cryptic words:

Here lies the soul of Count Louis Esterfield.

Year after year, travelers passed that stone, paying no notice to the inscription. One day, a man stopped in front of the tombstone and began digging. At last he came upon a metal box containing jewels, gold coins, and a note: "You are my heir," said the note. "I bequeath this wealth, to you who have understood. In this box is my soul—the money without which a man is but a machine and his life but a long procession of weary, empty years."

What folly! It is not money or the lack of money that makes the real difference in life. Only a relationship with God and a focus on spiritual realities makes life worth living.

The Special Gift to Caleb (14:1–15)

The account now turns to the distribution of the land west of the Jordan to the remaining nine and one-half tribes. The land was to be divided by lot. The Lord had told Moses that each tribe was to receive territory proportionate to its population, with the casting of lots to determine the location (Num. 26:54–56). According to Jewish tradition, the name of a tribe and the boundary lines of a territory were simultaneously drawn from two urns. This method designated each tribal inheritance. But it was not a matter of blind chance that decided tribal location, for God was superintending the whole procedure. The inequities of assignments that occurred, and which caused some tensions and jealousies among the tribes should have been accepted as a part of God's purpose and not something that was arbitrary and unfair.

And we, too, must accept our lot in life with gratitude and contentment. Some people think that everything in life should be equalized and made "fair," according to their definition of "fairness." But life is not fair and people are not equal in every respect. There are natural inequities in life. People are born with differences in intelligence, in physical appearance and abilities, in talent, in personality, in health, and in material advantages. In this life, we cannot understand the seeming unfairness of one child born with Downe's syndrome while another is born completely healthy. We cannot understand the unfairness of one child being born to live in a squalid, cockroach-infested housing project in "the 'hood" of South Central L.A., while another is born just a few miles away in Beverly Hills or Bel Air.

As Christians we know that our lot is not a matter of "luck" or "fate" or "fortune." Our lot is God's choice for our lives. Furthermore, we know that in the life to come, we will fully understand all the assignments God has made.

The time for the casting of lots arrived and the tribe of Judah assembled before Joshua in Gilgal to receive the first portion. Before the lots were cast, Caleb, the grand old man of Israel, stepped forward to remind Joshua of a promise the Lord made to him forty-five years earlier: "To him and to his sons I will give the land on which he has set foot because he has followed the Lord fully."[4]

William Hunt, the noted painter, once tutored a young pupil in the art of painting. As they stood in a field at dusk, the boy observed and painted the setting of the sun behind an old barn. Hunt looked over the boy's shoulder and noticed that the lad was concentrating on each individual shingle of the barn while ignoring the glories of the sunset. "Son!" the artist sternly admonished. "The sun is sinking fast! You haven't time for both shingles and sunsets! You must choose!"

Caleb was an old man. The sun was setting on his life and he, too, had to choose. What did he want most of all? In a remarkable address to Joshua, he reviewed the highlights of his life and made his request.

1. Kadesh-barnea (verses 6–9)

Caleb is introduced in this account as "the son of Jephunneh the Kenizzite." Genesis 15:19 tells us that the Kenizzites were a tribe of Canaan in Abraham's day. Caleb's family, then, was originally outside the covenant and commonwealth of Israel, as were Heber the Kenite, Ruth the Moabitess, Uriah the Hittite, and others. It is apparent that the Kenizzites, in part at least, joined the tribe of Judah before the Exodus. Their faith was not merely hereditary, but was the fruit of conviction. And Caleb displayed that faith throughout his long lifetime.

Standing before General Joshua—his old friend from their days as fellow spies and soldiers under the command of Moses—Caleb glowingly retold the story of that never-to-be forgotten day forty-five years earlier, when the two of them stood alone against the other ten spies and the cowardly mob. The other spies agreed that it was a beautiful and fruitful land, but concluded that Israel could never conquer it. Of all the twelve spies Moses had sent into Canaan, only Joshua and Caleb had faith to believe that Canaan could be conquered. But the people of Israel sided with the fears of the majority rather than with the faith of Joshua and Caleb. A national rebellion appeared imminent. Thus Israel shrank back in fear from the land and the prosperity God had promised. (See Numbers 13 and 14.)

But God singled out the two faithful spies for blessing. He made Joshua the commander of the successful campaign to lead Israel into the land of promise. And he singled Caleb out for blessing and special reward in the distribution of the land. (See Num. 14:24 and Deut. 1:36.)

Why did God honor Caleb in this way? *Because Caleb had honored God.* On that day, forty-five years earlier, Caleb had revealed himself as a man who completely trusted the goodness and the power of God. It was not that Caleb minimized the problems Israel faced. He fully recognized the opposition that would be posed by fierce men of gigantic stature, living within fortified cities. But Caleb had faith in a great God, a God who was bigger than any giant, and stronger than any city wall.

The problem with the other ten spies was that they looked at God through the wrong end of the telescope! They looked at God through the lens of their problems. By magnifying the problems and obstacles before them, *they minimized God!*

During World War II, German Pastor Martin Niemoller was imprisoned by the Nazis. Reflecting on his experience in the prison camps, he said,

> First the Nazis came for the Communists, and I did not speak up, for I was not a Communist. Then the

Nazis came for the Jews, and I did not speak up, for I was not a Jew. Then the Nazis came for the Trade Unionists, and I did not speak up, for I was not a Trade Unionist. And then the Nazis came for the Catholics, and I did not speak up, for I was a Protestant. And then the Nazis came for me. By that time, there was no one left to speak up for anyone.

At Kadesh-barnea, Caleb spoke up for God. May we have the courage to speak up as Caleb did, even though we may be part of a small and shrinking minority in an increasingly hostile world.

2. The Wilderness and Conquest (verses 10–11)

Caleb reminisced about God's faithfulness to him over many years. First he affirmed that God had kept him alive during the past forty-five years, just as He had promised. Indeed, Caleb was the recipient of *two* divine promises: one, that his life would be prolonged; and the other, that he would one day inherit the territory he had bravely explored near Hebron. Alexander Maclaren noted that "the daily fulfillment of the one fed the fire of his faith in the ultimate accomplishment of the other."[5]

Forty-five years is a long time to wait for the fulfillment of a pledge, a long time for faith to live on a promise. Yet Caleb's faith was strong enough to hang on through the long, exhausting years of the wilderness wanderings and the demanding years of the conquest. *Caleb had an unshakeable faith in the promises of God.* Those promises sustained him in the difficult times. God's promises are sufficient to sustain you and me as well. As David Adeney writes,

> I discovered the power of the Word of God in my own life during a time of depression when I was strongly

tempted to give up. Almost in desperation, I turned to
John's Gospel and read it all through at one sitting. God
spoke to me through it and I realized again that faith
comes through hearing of the Word of Christ.[6]

Bible historians take special note of Caleb's statement
in 14:10 because it enables us to determine how long it
took Israel to conquer Canaan. Caleb stated that he was
forty years old when he went to spy out the land. The wilderness wanderings lasted thirty-eight years, giving a total
of seventy-eight years. Caleb is now eighty-five, which
means the conquest lasted seven years. This is confirmed
by Caleb's reference in verse 10 to God's sustaining grace
for forty-five years since Kadesh-barnea—thirty-eight
years of wandering plus seven years of conquest.

There is a deep tragedy here when we see that the
Israelites could have possessed their homeland in about
eight years if they had responded in faith to Caleb and
Joshua at Kadesh-barnea. Instead it took *forty-five
years*, because the unbelieving generation was sentenced
to die in the wilderness. What price unbelief!

3. Hebron (verses 12–15)

Caleb concluded his speech to Joshua with an
astounding request. At the age of eighty-five, when he
might have asked for a quiet place to spend his last days,
doing a little gardening or playing checkers, he requested
instead the section of land which had struck fear into the
hearts of the ten unbelieving spies. This was the inheritance he desired in fulfillment of God's earlier promise.
And though old age is usually a time when people are
more eager to talk about old battles than to take on new
ones, Caleb was ready for one more good fight! He was
eager to confront the Anakim at Hebron and to take the
city for his possession.

It has been said that you can always tell a man's size by the size of the challenge he undertakes. Caleb chose a large and ominous challenge—not because he arrogantly trusted in his own ability, *but because he believed that a good and powerful God was at his side!* When he said, "Perhaps the Lord will be with me," he was expressing humility, not doubt. Then, with a voice strong with confidence and with eyes flashing with determination, he concluded, "I shall drive them out, as the Lord has spoken." And drive them out he did, as we read in Joshua 15:13–19.

Joshua's response to his old friend is captured in this fictionalized dialogue, as suggested by Gene Getz:

> Caleb, it's yours. You deserve it. I'm sorry I forgot! It is because of you that I mustered enough courage to stand against Israel's hostility and disobedience. It is because of you that I spoke out against their rebellion and unbelief. You helped me become the man that I am—a man that God could trust to lead Israel in place of Moses. I drew strength from you, Caleb. And you have been faithful to me. You never showed jealousy or resentment because you were not chosen to lead Israel—even though you were a stronger man than I, both physically and emotionally. I'm sorry I didn't remember God's promise myself. I'm glad you reminded me! It's yours! Take the mountain God promised you![7]

By choosing a hazardous and hard mission over a well-deserved life of ease, Caleb reminds us of the many Christian leaders—servants of Jesus Christ—who forsook the comfortable life to go where God directed. A notable example is William Borden, whose life was described in these words by a Dallas Seminary student:

He couldn't have done anything else—or could he?

• While a student at Yale University, he was elected president of his Phi Beta Kappa chapter.

• At 20, he founded the effective Yale Hope Rescue Mission.

• Shortly after Graduation from Princeton Seminary, he spoke to no fewer than thirty leading colleges and seminaries within a period of three months.

• He became a millionaire, as heir to the Borden Dairy fortune.

So what did he decide to do with his life?

• He dedicated himself to reach the Moslems in an interior province of China. He went to Cairo to learn Arabic and to take studies in Islam in anticipation of this work. Within a few months he was dead from cerebral meningitis.

Why did he do this?

• He wrote: "In every man's heart there is a throne and a cross. If Christ is on the throne, self is on the cross; and if self, even a little bit, is on the throne, Jesus is on the cross in that man's heart. . . . If Jesus is on the throne, you will go where He wants you to go."

• He prayed: "Lord Jesus, I take hands off, as far as my life is concerned. I put Thee on the throne in my heart. Change, cleanse, use me as Thou shalt choose. I thank Thee."

Was it worth it?

• He did extensive tract distribution and personal work, and organized others to do the same.

• Through his death, many dedicated themselves to carry the Gospel to those who had not heard it.

• His testimony has been greatly used among Moslems to show what Christian love led one man to do for them.

The Portion of the Tribe of Judah (15:1–63)

Caleb's request having been granted, the people returned to the business of dividing the land west of the Jordan among the nine and one-half tribes. Judah was the first to receive an inheritance and as the largest tribe, their portion exceeded that of any of the others. The land allotment after the conquest is a remarkable fulfillment of Jacob's prophecy regarding Judah and his seed in Genesis 49:8–11:

"Judah, your brothers shall praise you;
Your hand shall be on the neck of your enemies;
Your father's sons shall bow down to you.
Judah is a lion's whelp;
From the prey, my son, you have gone up.
He crouches, he lies down as a lion,
And as a lion, who dares rouse him up?
The scepter shall not depart from Judah,
Nor the ruler's staff from between his feet,
Until Shiloh comes,
And to him shall be the obedience of the peoples.
He ties his foal to the vine,
And his donkey's colt to the choice vine;
He washes his garments in wine,
And his robes in the blood of grapes."

We see the fulfillment of Jacob's prophecy regarding Judah in the following facts arising out of the allotment of land to the tribe of Judah:

• Judah was surrounded by enemies. The Moabites were on the east, Edomites on the south, Amalekites to the southwest, and Philistines to the west. Thus hemmed in by fierce foes, Judah would need strong rulers—"lions" like David—in order to survive.

• The land allotted to Judah was ideally suited to the

planting of vineyards. It was from a Judean valley that the spies cut down the gigantic cluster of grapes.

• Judah was the tribe from which Messiah would come. He would come as Shiloh, the Man of rest (Matt. 11:28), or the Peace-Bringer (Isa. 9:6).

The borders of Judah are described in Joshua 15:1–12. The southern boundary extended from the south end of the Dead Sea westward to the river of Egypt (Wadi el-Arish). The northern border extended from the north tip of the Dead Sea to the Mediterranean. These two bodies of water were the eastern and western limits. Composed mainly of the territory conquered by Joshua in his southern campaign (Josh. 10), the area included some fertile tracts, but large parts were mountainous and barren.

Included in Judah's portion was Hebron which had been granted to Caleb. Verses 15 through 19 record how Caleb, with the aid of a warrior named Othniel, claimed and enlarged this inheritance. Caleb rewarded Othniel by offering him his daughter Achsah to marry, thus making Othniel his son-in-law.

The cities of Judah are listed according to their location in the four main geographic regions of the tribe: the cities in the south or Negev (verses 21–32); the cities in the western foothills or Shephelah (verses 33–47); the cities in the central hill country (verses 48–60); the cities in the sparsely populated wilderness of Judah which slopes down toward the Dead Sea (verses 61–62).

Judah inherited well over a hundred cities and seems to have occupied them with little or no difficulty, with the significant exception of Jerusalem. "As for the Jebusites," says verse 63, "the inhabitants of Jerusalem, the sons of Judah could not drive them out."

Was it that the men of Judah *could not* or *would not*? Was the failure due to a lack of strength or a lack of faith? And what does this statement mean to you and me, as we contemplate all the things we say we "can't" do? As Charles Swindoll points out, we often say we "can't" do something when the truth is that we *won't* do it. He writes,

> *Can't* and *won't*. Christians need to be very careful which one they choose. It seems that we prefer to use *can't*.
> "I just *can't* get along with my wife."
> "My husband and I *can't* communicate."
> "I *can't* discipline the kids like I should."
> "I just *can't* give up the affair I'm having."
> "I *can't* stop overeating."
> "I *can't* find the time to pray."
> "I *can't* quit gossiping." . . .
> Hey, let's face it, we don't because we won't . . . we disobey because we want to, not because we have to . . . because we choose to, not because we're forced to. The sooner we are willing to own up realistically to our responsibility and stop playing the blame game at pity parties for ourselves, the more we'll learn and change, and the less we'll burn and blame.[8]

The Christian's answer to the question "Can't or won't?" is found in Philippians 4:13—"I can do all things through Him who strengthens me." It is hard, therefore, to believe that the men of Judah could not call upon this same strength to push the Jebusites out of Jerusalem. The account of Judah's inheritance ends on an ominous note: "so the Jebusites live with the sons of Judah at Jerusalem until this day." As H. Forbes Witherby observes,

> They could not drive them out! The note has been struck, its tone will increase in volume, it will repeat itself again and again, until the sound of victory be swallowed up in the cries of defeat and loss and in the wails of bondage and ruin.[9]

The Portion of the Joseph Tribes
(16:1–17:18)

The powerful house of Joseph, made up of the tribes of Ephraim and Manasseh, inherited the rich territory of central Canaan. Because Joseph kept the family alive during the famine in Egypt, the patriarch Jacob ordained that the two sons of Joseph, Ephraim and Manasseh, should be made founders and heads of tribes with their uncles (Gen. 48:5). Their lot in Canaan was in many respects the most beautiful and fertile.

1. The tribe of Ephraim (16:4–10)

Located immediately north of the territory to be assigned to Dan and Benjamin, Ephraim's allotment stretched from the Jordan to the Mediterranean. It included the sites of some of Joshua's battles, as well as Shiloh, where the tabernacle would remain for some 300 years. To encourage unity, some of Ephraim's cities were located in the territory of Manasseh.

But the men of Ephraim, like those of Judah, did not completely drive out the Canaanites from their region. Motivated by a materialistic attitude, they chose to put the Canaanites under tribute—exacting payments from them on an annual basis—in order to gain additional wealth. That proved to be a fatal mistake, for in later centuries, in the time of the Judges, the arrangement was reversed as the Canaanites rose up and enslaved the Israelites.

In addition to the historical lesson, there is a spiritual principle here. It is all too easy to tolerate and excuse some pet sin in our lives, only to wake up someday to the grim realization that it has risen up to possess us and drive us to spiritual defeat. It pays to deal with sin decisively and completely.

2. The Tribe of Manasseh (17:1–13)

The descendants of the firstborn of Manasseh settled in Transjordan. The remaining heirs settled in Canaan proper and were given the territory north of Ephraim, extending also from the Jordan River to the Mediterranean Sea.

Special note was taken of the daughters of Zelophehad. Because the father died without sons, the Lord had declared that in this and other such cases the daughters could receive the inheritance (Num. 27:1–11). They now claimed and received their portion within the territory of Manasseh. The incident is not without significance, for it shows an elevated concern and respect for women, at a time when most societies regarded women as mere property.

Several cities located in the tribes of Issachar and Asher were given to Manasseh. These were the Canaanite fortresses of Bethshean, Ibleam, Dor, Endor, Taanach, and Megiddo. Apparently it was considered necessary for military purposes that these cities be held by a strong tribe. The decision however was in vain, for the sons of Manasseh, like the Ephraimites, chose tribute over triumph.

3. The Complaint of Ephraim and Manasseh (verses 14–18)

The sons of Joseph registered a belligerent complaint with Joshua, claiming that their allotment was too small for such a large population. With tact and firmness, Joshua challenged them first to clear the trees and settle in the forested hill country. Then they should combine their energies to drive out the Canaanites.

But this is not what they wanted to hear. In 17:16, the sons of Joseph protested, "The hill country is not enough for us, and all the Canaanites who live in the valley land have chariots of iron." In other words, "Joshua, your solution is no good! It's still not fair! It's going to be too hard for us to clear out both the trees and the Canaanites! We want choice, developed, ready-to-occupy real estate! We don't want a 'fixer-upper'! That's too much work!" As Francis Schaeffer notes,

> The people of God did not go on to do what God told them to do for two reasons. First they wanted peace at any cost and in spite of God's commands; second, they wanted wealth. They were practical materialists. For sake of ease and money, they did not go forward and do what God told them to do. . . .
>
> We Christians stand in the same danger. It is all too easy to fail to possess the possessions God has promised because we either draw back out of fear of the troubles that being a Christian will bring us or we become caught up in the affluent society where people sail their little boats upon this plastic culture.[10]

Better by far to follow the model of Caleb, whose driving ambition was not acquiring ease and wealth, but *doing the will of God*, regardless of the cost in possessions and peace. Caleb followed this godly ambition to the very end. His vision and purpose are summed up in these lines by Amy Carmichael:

> Make us Thy mountaineers;
> We would not linger on the lower slope,
> Fill us afresh with hope, O God of hope,
> That undefeated we may climb the hill
> As seeing Him who is invisible.
> Let us die climbing. When this little while
> Lies far behind us, and the last defile
> Is all alight, and in that light we see
> Our Leader and our Lord, what will it be?[11]

In these pages of the book of Joshua, we have seen God, the Divine Realtor, at work. The lists of names and families and places may make for dry reading on the surface, but embedded within these chapters is the drama of a nation staking out its place in the world, the climactic moment when a wandering people finally come into a land and say, "This is home! Now we can rest!"

For us, a land of promise still awaits. But someday we will walk upon that land. We will survey it with our eyes, drink in its beauty, and breathe in its fragrance. Some day, we too will take possession of a land that has been purchased and deeded over to us by the same Divine Realtor who was with Joshua, Caleb, and the tribes of Israel. The land God has for us is in escrow right now, but the closing takes place soon. You and I can take possession just as soon as we go to meet the Lord. And when that day comes, we too will say, "Ah, this is home! At last, we can rest!"

QUESTIONS FOR REFLECTION AND DISCUSSION

See Your Own Reflection

1. Do you think of the house or apartment you live in now as "home"? Or when you hear the word "home" do you think back to a previous dwelling place? Or some future "home" of your dreams? What is "home" to you?

Dig a Little Deeper

2. Why did the Levites receive no territory as an inheritance? How do you think the Levites felt as they saw all the other tribes receiving huge pieces of real

estate? If you had been a Levite, would you have felt cheated or honored by this settlement? Explain your answer.

3. How would you describe Caleb's character?

What qualities do you see in Caleb that you wish you had more of in your own life?

Caleb was a man of strength, courage, ambition, and energy at eighty-five years of age. How do you account for that? Do you think you can have those qualities when you are eighty-five? Why or why not?

4. Why were the portions of Caleb and his family not determined by lot like the rest? Was this preferential treatment fair or unfair to the other tribes and families? Explain your answer.

5. What do you think about the way Caleb chose a husband for his daughter?

What did Othniel later become? (See Judges 3:7–11.)

6. Joseph's descendents were dissatisfied with the allotments of land they received. Were they right or wrong to feel this way?

Joshua attempted to resolve the dissatisfaction of the tribes of Ephraim and Manasseh. What was his solution? Why wouldn't they accept it?

Let's Get Personal

7. What have you received as an inheritance from the Lord? How have you handled and used that inheritance?

8. What is your "lot in life"? Are you thankful or resentful over your "lot in life"?

To whom do you give credit or blame for your "lot in life"? Your parents? Your mate? Some other person? God? Yourself?

Can your "lot in life" be improved? If not, why not? Is the real answer that you "can't" improve it or that you "won't"?

If you *can* improve your "lot in life," *how* would you go about doing so?

10

GOD'S INHERITANCE— NO ONE LEFT OUT

JOSHUA 18–21

Quitting is easy. Anybody can say, "The hill is too high," or, "This job is too hard." Anybody can say, "I'm tired," or, "I'm bored," or, "I'm scared." But a Christian leader isn't just "anybody." A leader commits himself to the challenge he has accepted. A leader doesn't take a job half-way. A leader doesn't quit. A leader sees it through.

Israel stopped in the middle. Although much of Canaan had been allocated, seven tribes were still without a home —and they were apparently content to continue a nomadic and purposeless existence.

But Joshua was a *leader.* He saw the moral and practical danger in doing things half-way. The willingness of Israel to settle for less than God's best was totally unacceptable to Joshua. So he prodded his people into finishing the job they had started.

The Portions of the Remaining Tribes (18:1–19:48)

Before the final divisions of the land were made, the Israelites moved *en masse* from Gilgal to Shiloh, from the Jordan Valley to the hill country. Shiloh was located in the center of the land, and in this central and convenient location the tabernacle was erected.

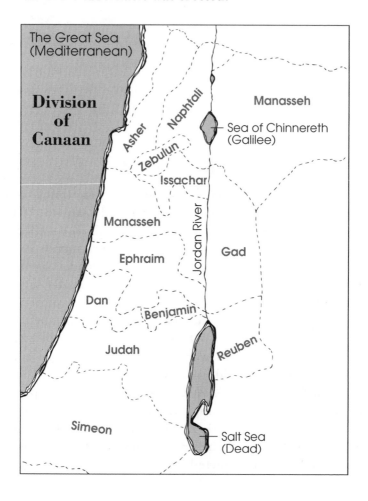

The dissatisfaction of the sons of Joseph with their allotment was an ominous foreshadowing of the future disintegration of the nation because of self-interest. To counteract such a tendency, the tabernacle was set up in Shiloh to promote a sense of national unity. It also served as a reminder to the people that the key to prosperity and blessing in the land was worship of Jehovah.

Worship is what held life together for the people and the nation of Israel. In fact, every nation or community which has experienced a genuine sense of cohesiveness and purpose has been a nation or community which was built upon a foundation of worship. As one Puritan said, "Wherever I have a house, there God shall have an altar."

But the concept of the centrality of God in human life has fallen on hard times in our own era. As Professor Arthur Holmes observes,

> The bits and pieces of a man's life pull him in a hundred directions, unless he has within himself something to hold them together. But our day has no integrating world-view. There was a time when the religious outlook unified life in Western society. Think of the British or European countryside: the first sign of an approaching town is the church spire that soars above everything else and around which, it seems, the whole community once clustered. In place of this we now have the high-rise, the factory belt, or the corn silo, symbols of our materialism, or the sprawling metropolis that has no unifying theme unless it be the decentralized existence of fragmented man.[1]

When the Israelites assembled for the celebration of the new worship center, Joshua sensed that a feeling of war-weariness had overtaken them. They were exhausted in the struggle for the conquest of Canaan, yet Joshua sharply reproached them. Joshua asks in 18:33, "How long will you put off entering to take possession of the land which the Lord, the God of your fathers, has given you?" It was apparently the responsibility of the tribes to initiate matters relating to allocation of territory. Every passing day was a day lost in the program of completely occupying the land, and a day in which the enemy could return or become more firmly entrenched.

Joshua was for action, but not before careful preparations were made. As we saw in the previous chapter, Joshua has moved from a role of visionary military commander into a role of manager-administrator. Here we see him carrying out that role in much the same way a top-level manager at Ford or IBM or AT&T would: In 18:3–6, we see that Joshua set the objectives, organized and defined the work needed to meet that objective, and assigned the work to a team of people who were accountable to him for their performance. Specifically, he appointed a commission of twenty-one skilled men—three from each of seven tribes—and sent them to make a topographical survey of the remaining land. At the conclusion of this task, the team of surveyors was accountable to report back to Joshua with their findings.

This complex task required time and skill. The Jewish historian Josephus states that these men were experts in geometry, and it is probable that they had mastered the science of land surveying as young men in Egypt. Who among them dreamed that they would ever put that knowledge to use so strategically in their own land of promise? There is a lesson here for you and me: God has a way of taking the seemingly disconnected and useless bits and pieces of our experience and putting them to good use in our lives—*if* we offer them all to Him!

After writing their expert observations in a book, the surveyors returned to Shiloh where Joshua proceeded to cast lots to determine the portions of territory to be allotted to the seven remaining tribes.

1. The Territory of Benjamin (18:11–28)

By the hand of God, Benjamin was assigned the land that lay between Judah and Ephraim, which helped to cool the simmering rivalry between these two leading tribes. While the area was covered by mountains and ravines, extending only twenty-five miles from east to west, and fifteen miles at its widest point from north to south, it included many cities important to biblical history—Jericho, Bethel, Gibeon, Ramah, Mizpeh, and Jerusalem. Thus the ultimate site of the temple was in Benjamin, fulfilling Moses' prophecy. (See Deut. 33:12.)

2. The Territory of Simeon (19:1–9)

In fulfillment of Jacob's prophecy (Gen. 49:5–7), and because Judah could not cope with the large area assigned to her, Simeon was given land in the southern section of Judah's territory. But it was not long before Simeon lost individuality as a tribe, for the territory of this tribe was eventually incorporated into Judah, and many Simeonites migrated north to Ephraim and Manasseh (2 Chron. 15:9; 34:6). This explains how, after the division of the kingdom following Solomon, there were ten tribes in the north and only two—Judah and Benjamin —in the south.

3. The Territory of Zebulun (19:10–16)

According to Jacob's prophecy, Zebulun would "dwell at the seashore; and . . . be a haven for ships" (Gen. 49:13). This tribe was assigned a portion in lower Galilee, which many consider to have been landlocked; however, a strip of land extended to the Mediterranean

Sea forming an enclave in Issachar's territory. The city of Nazareth was within the borders of Zebulun's allotment.

4. The Territory of Issachar (19:17–23)

Lying east of Zebulun and south of the Sea of Galilee, Issachar was to occupy the fertile and beautiful valley of Jezreel, also a noted battlefield. Until the time of David, however, the people of this tribe remained in the mountainous district on the eastern end of the valley.

5. The Territory of Asher (19:24–31)

Asher was assigned the Mediterranean coastal lands from Mt. Carmel north to Tyre and Sidon. By virtue of Asher's vital position, this tribe was to protect Israel from northern coastal enemies such as the Phoenicians. By David's time, Asher had faded into insignificance, though the identity of this once-great tribe was not lost. Anna the prophetess, who along with Simeon gave thanks for the birth of Jesus (see Luke 2:36–38), was from the tribe of Asher.

6. The Territory of Naphtali (19:32–39)

Adjacent to Asher on the east, Naphtali had the Jordan River and Sea of Galilee as its eastern boundary. While not highly significant in the Old Testament period, Naphtali occupied lands that were important in New Testament history because the Galilean ministry of Jesus Christ was centered there. The Prophet Isaiah contrasted the early gloom (caused by an Assyrian invasion) with the later glory of this district:

> But there will be no more gloom for her who was in anguish; in earlier times He treated the land of Zebulun and the land of Naphtali with contempt, but later on He shall make it glorious, by the way of the sea, on the

other side of Jordan, Galilee of the Gentiles. The people who walk in darkness will see a great light; those who live in a dark land, the light will shine on them.[2]

7. The Territory of Dan (19:40–48)

It appears that the least desirable portion of the land fell to the tribe of Dan. Surrounded by Ephraim and Benjamin on the north and east, and by Judah on the south, Dan's boundaries coincided with theirs. There were cities but no fertile, productive lands included in Dan's portion. Not only was the original tract of land too small, but when part of the territory of Dan was lost to the Amorites (see Jud. 1:34), the majority of the tribe migrated to the far north, settling in Leshem (Laish), opposite the northern sector of Naphtali.

Thus God provided for the needs of each tribe. Though in some cases a part of the inheritance was still in the hands of the enemy, the Israelites were to possess it by faith, trusting God to enable them to defeat their foes. Failing to do so would mean poverty and weakness, conditions God did not plan for His people.

A number of years ago, newspapers carried the story of a search on Chicago's skid row for a British man who was the sole heir to $12 million. The poor man's situation was tragic—he had access to great wealth, but being unaware of the heritage that awaited him, he was living in abject poverty. Israel faced that same danger—and so do we, unless we appropriate by faith the spiritual blessings God intends us to have as Christians.

The Special Provision for Joshua (19:49–51)

Whereas Caleb's inheritance was determined first, Joshua's was last! Only after all the tribes had received their allotments did Joshua ask for his. What a selfless spirit this man demonstrated! And what a contrast his behavior provides to many of the leaders of our own time, who use their position and influence to line their own pockets.

Joshua's choice of land further revealed his humility. He asked for Timnath-serah, a city in the rugged, infertile, mountainous district of his own tribe. He could have appropriated land in the fairest and most productive area of Canaan. With deep appreciation for his godly leadership, the sons of Israel granted Joshua his modest request, and, says verse 50, "he built the city "—that is, he added to it— "and settled in it. "

Thus in one of the final pictures of this stalwart leader, we see that Joshua was not only a warrior but also a builder. That combination is a rare one among God's servants.

The late Rev. William McCarrell, for many years the dedicated pastor of the Cicero Bible Church of Cicero, Illinois, was a fighter in the Joshua mold. On one occasion, he confronted the faculty of a nearby university, challenging them face to face regarding their unscriptural teachings. He said he felt like Daniel in the lions' den.

Another time he returned from lunch to discover that one of Al Capone's henchmen had delivered a cash contribution to the church's office. With money in hand, McCarrell strode the few blocks to Capone's headquarters and tossed the contribution on the desk, declaring that he could not under any circumstances accept their donation.

But McCarrell was also a builder in the Joshua mold. Beginning with a small, struggling congregation, he built a dynamic and flourishing church. Yet that was not enough. Reaching out to other communities, he established more than twenty other Bible-teaching churches, several of which have grown to significant size. As both a fighter and a builder, William McCarrell was a modern-day Joshua.

The Assignment of the Cities of Refuge (20:1–9)

The law given to Moses provided for the future establishment of cities of refuge (Ex. 21:13). These cities, providing a haven for the unintentional manslayer, are dealt with in detail in Numbers 35 and Deuteronomy 19.

The fact that these cities are discussed in four books of the Old Testament suggests that the subject is of great importance. God wished to impress upon Israel the sanctity of human life. To take another person's life, even if unintentionally, is a very serious thing.

In the ancient world, blood revenge was widely practiced. When a person was killed, his nearest relative took responsibility for vengeance. The vendetta was often handed down from one generation to another, so that larger and larger numbers of innocent people died violently. William Blaikie tells of a section of Italy in which, over a period of four centuries, more than 600,000 people were wounded or murdered out of revenge.[3] It is not hard to see why cities of refuge were necessary in the ancient world.

A clear distinction is made in the Old Testament between premeditated murder and accidental manslaughter (Num. 35:11–16). In the case of murder, the nearest kinsman became the avenger of blood, responsible to avenge the crime by killing the guilty party. If a man killed another person accidentally, he was provided a place of asylum in one of six cities of refuge (20:3). But he was to hurry to the nearest shelter without delay. According to Jewish tradition, the roads leading to the cities were kept in excellent condition and the crossroads were well marked with signposts reading, "Refuge! Refuge!" Runners were also stationed along the way to guide the fugitive.

Having arrived at the gate, the manslayer was to present his case (no doubt, breathlessly and without any wasted words!) to the elders of the city, who formed an ancient court of law. (See Deut. 21:19; 22:15.) A provisional decision would then be made to grant him asylum until such time as a trial could be held. Preferably, that trial took place before representatives of the community nearest to the scene of the killing. If acquitted of premeditated murder, the manslayer was returned to the city of refuge where he lived until the death of the high priest, after which he was free to return to his home.

Many have puzzled over the meaning of the death of the high priest in relation to the change in the status of the manslayer. It seems best to view it simply as a change in priestly administration which served as a statute of limitations ending the fugitive's exile in the city of refuge.

The six designated cities were located on both sides of the Jordan River. On the west side were Kadesh in Galilee, Shechem in Ephraim, and Hebron in Judah. The cities on the east side were Bezer in the south, Ramoth in the region of Gilead, and Golan in the northern territory of Bashan.

We do not read any anecdotal accounts in the Old Testament of a single instance in which this merciful provision was utilized. Some critics suggest that the silence of Scripture indicates these cities were not part of the Mosaic legislation but a provision instituted after the exile. Yet the post-exilic books likewise contain no reference to their use, and so it is further suggested by other critics that they were not occupied until the time of Christ.

In the face of such shifting arguments, it is much better to recognize the historicity of these accounts and explain the silence of the record by the obvious fact that the scriptural authors were selective about what they recorded. It was apparently more important to the writers (and the Author) of Scripture that the existence of that provision be mentioned than it was to document specific cases of the use of that provision.

Some Christians claim that the provision of the cities of refuge is a symbolic type of the believer's salvation in Christ. These sanctuaries do remind us of Psalm 46:1: "God is our Refuge and Strength, a very present help in time of trouble;" and of Romans 8:1: "There is therefore now no condemnation for those who are in Christ Jesus." And the writer of the Epistle to the Hebrews must have had the Old Testament cities of refuge in mind when he wrote that believers have strong encouragement, having "fled for refuge in laying hold of the hope set before us."[4]

We may properly conclude, then, that the cities of refuge are typical of Christ to whom the sinner may flee for refuge when pursued by the avenging law—the law of God which decrees judgment and death for all who commit sin. In fact, the key expression which is found again and again in the New Testament epistles—"in Christ"—may also be an echo of the refuge which these cities provided. For in Christ, there is safety and security for every believer.

One of the most impressive art masterpieces in the world is Michelangelo's painting of the Last Judgment, on the ceiling of the Sistine Chapel in Rome. The focus of the painting is Jesus Christ, who appears in His role as the implacable Judge. Viewers are struck with awe and feelings of deep emotion as they consider the inevitable day of reckoning that lies ahead of the entire human race. Michelangelo himself was filled with anxiety and dread as he worked on this painting, realizing his own unworthiness to stand before God.

But no person needs to fear the judgment to come, because Christ has made a way of escape available to everyone, without exception. For those who flee to Christ for refuge, there is forgiveness, peace, hope, and eternal life.

The Appointment of Levitical Cities (21:1–45)

In the last and crowning act of distribution, the leaders of the tribe of Levi stepped forward to claim the cities which had been promised to them by Moses. (See Num. 35:1–8.) These forty-eight cities, with pastureland, were assigned to the Levites, and included the six cities of refuge. The three main branches of the tribe of Levi were named for Levi's three sons—Kohath, Gershon, and Merari.

The Kohathites had twenty-three cities for the priests, the descendants of Aaron. Thirteen of these cities were located among the tribes of Judah, Benjamin, and Simeon. The other ten were located in Ephraim, Dan, and western Manasseh for the other branches of the Kohathites. Thus the priestly cities fell ultimately within the southern kingdom of Judah. Eventually, the temple would be built in the capital of Judah, Jerusalem.

The Gershonite cities were located in eastern Manasseh, Issachar, Asher, and Naphtali. Merari received cities in Zebulun and among the Transjordanian tribes of Reuben and Gad.

This scattering of the tribe of Levi among the other tribes marked the fulfillment of Jacob's curse on Levi, along with Simeon, for their senseless murder of the Shechemites (Gen. 49:5,7). In the case of Levi's descendants, God overruled to preserve their tribal identity and make them a blessing to all Israel. He did this because the Levites stood with Moses at a time of acute crisis (Ex. 32:26) and because Phinehas, a Levite, vindicated God's righteous name in the plains of Moab (Num. 25).

But at the time of the assignment, many of the cities were under Canaanite control and had to be conquered. The Levites did not always succeed in battle, and the other tribes did not offer to help. This would appear to be the simplest explanation for the lack of complete correlation between the list of levitical cities here and in 1 Chronicles 6:54–81.

The potential for good in the dispersion of Levites among the other tribes was almost unlimited. Moses, in his final blessing of the tribes, said of the Levites, "They shall teach Thine ordinances to Jacob, and Thy law to Israel."[5] The solemn responsibility and high privilege of the Levites was to instruct Israel in the law of the Lord and to maintain the knowledge of His Word among the people. Especially in the north and east, the Levites ought to have been barriers against the idolatry of Tyre and Sidon, and the heathen practices of the desert tribes and Damascus.

It has been estimated that no one in Israel lived more than ten miles from a city in which Levites had their residence. Thus every Israelite was close to a man well-versed in the Law of Moses, someone who could give advice and counsel on the many problems of religious, family, and political life. It was essential that Israel obey the Word of God in all areas of life; without this their prosperity would cease and their privileges would be forfeited.

The Levites did not live up to their potential or fulfill their mission. As William Blaikie notes, "If the Levites had all been consecrated men, idolatry and its great brood of corruptions would never have spread over the land of Israel."[6]

In 1962, when Eddie Arcaro retired as one of the nation's most successful horse-jockies, a reporter asked him if he still got up early to walk his mounts around the track while the dew was still on the ground. Arcaro frankly confessed, "It becomes difficult to get up early once a guy starts wearing silk pajamas." Perhaps too many of the Levites succumbed—as Eddie Arcaro did, and as many of us do—to the softening influences of "the good life."

All the territory of the Promised Land had been allocated. God had kept His promise to give the people of Israel the land, rest on every side, and victory over their enemies. The Lord faithfully performed every part of His obligation. This is not to say that at any given time, every corner of the land was in Israel's possession. God Himself had told Israel they would conquer the land gradually (see Deut. 7:22). Nor can we ignore the tragedies that developed in the period of the Judges—tragedies which were directly due to Israel's sin.

Yet the unfaithfulness of Israel cannot diminish the faithfulness of God. Paul reminds us of this fact in his words to Timothy: "If we are faithless, He remains faithful; for He cannot deny Himself."[7] And the book of Joshua affirms this fact in the last verse of chapter 22: "Not one of the good promises which the Lord had made to the house of Israel failed; all came to pass."

At this point in the story of Joshua, Israel did indeed occupy the land as God had promised. God does keep His word. "The promises of God," says Paul, "in Him they are yes."[8] Joshua trusted in God to fulfill what He promised, and Joshua was not disappointed.

God's promises to us are just as sure.

QUESTIONS FOR REFLECTION AND DISCUSSION

See Your Own Reflection

1. As this section of the book of Joshua opens, Joshua is impatient with the Israelites because they have not completed the job of giving every tribe a homeland. Are there unfinished tasks in your life—important jobs that never get more than half-way done? What are the distractions which sidetrack you? What will it take for you to get these jobs done?

Dig a Little Deeper

2. What was the task Joshua gave to the surveyors? Why did Joshua appoint surveyors from every tribe?

Was it fair for the land to be divided up by lots?

3. Notice the different decision-making styles that are mixed throughout these chapters. There is very decisive and deliberate planning involved in the surveying of the land. But there is also allotment by chance. There is the recognition of God's express command and prophecy in many of these decisions, but there is also the operation of human desires and demands.

Which of these means of decision-making do you consider the most valid in the context of Joshua's time?

Which of these decision-making approaches do you consider the most valid today—in your family, in your business, and in your church?

4. What is the significance of the placement of the "cities of refuge"? Do you think this concept was a good idea? Does it indicate that God is "soft on crime"? Do you think people probably took advantage of the system who were not entitled to? Do you think people who should have been sheltered were unable to make it to a "city of refuge?" In your opinion, was this system fair? Explain your answers.

Do you see any principles in the "city of refuge" concept that should be applied in the criminal justice practices of our own society? Do you think the way we deal with crime and punishment issues today is better or worse than the way they were dealt with in Joshua's day? Explain.

Do you see your church as a "city of refuge" for people who are in trouble or in danger? Explain.

Do you see your family as a "city of refuge" for people who are in trouble or in danger? Explain.

5. Who were the Levites and why were they special?

How do you think the other tribes reacted to the special treatment they received, and the cities they were given? How would you have reacted if you had been from one of the other tribes?

Let's Get Personal

7. The last verse in chapter 21 says that all of God's promises to the house of Israel were fulfilled. In your own experience, do you feel that God honors all of His promises? Why or why not?

8. What are some of the good things God has given you in the past three months?

11

THE DANGER OF MISJUDGING MOTIVES

JOSHUA 22

In the beautiful lake country of England, there is a point of land overlooking a lakeshore. That promontory is called Point Rash Judgment. It got its name many years ago when the poet William Wordsworth, his sister, and his friend and fellow poet Samuel Taylor Coleridge were walking along the shore. As they reached this point, they saw a man in a small boat, fishing out on the lake.

Since it was the season when all able-bodied men should have been out working in the harvest, the poets harshly criticized the man in the boat for his laziness in shirking his duties while other men were laboring in the fields. But as they continued walking and drawing closer, it became clear that the man was not able-bodied at all. He was old and infirm. They had misjudged him.

On that day, Wordsworth and Coleridge named that promontory "Point Rash Judgment"—a name which has stuck till this day.

Rash judgment is a dangerous thing. It can divide friend from friend and brother from brother. It can destroy reputations. It can ruin lives. It can destroy churches.

Pastor Wilkins (not his real name) shepherds a medium-sized congregation. He was enjoying a successful ministry at that church until trouble struck. One of his elders came to him and said, "Pastor, I think you should know that a number of rumors are going around about you. I thought I owed it to you to talk to you face-to-face and ask you if they are true." The elder then listed the rumors—rumors concerning off-color jokes he had allegedly told; rumors concerning alleged financial indiscretions; rumors concerning alleged dishonesty; rumors about his wife and children.

The pastor first turned white with shock as he listened—then red with anger. None of the rumors were true! "*Why,*" this pastor wondered aloud, "after several years of successful ministry, was someone now circulating lies about himself and his family?"

"Look," replied the elder, "this rumor-mongering is destructive, and it is sin. We can't just sit on this situation. We have to be pro-active." So he and Pastor Wilkins proceeded to track the path of the rumors. People known to have spread the rumors were visited by the pastor and the elder, and they were asked what they had been told and by whom. Pastor Wilkins told each person, "I give you my word as your pastor that none of these stories is true. And I would like you to promise me that if you ever encounter such a story again, that you would come to me and ask me about it rather than passing it along to another person."

As they investigated, Pastor Wilkins and the elder discovered that the minds of over a hundred parishioners had been infected by the rumors, and many people were now openly opposed to this pastor's ministry. Several said, "Pastor Wilkins has to go!" A church split was in the making. It is a curious quirk of human nature that even people who had been Pastor Wilkins' staunchest supporters were suddenly ready to believe the worst about him!

Eventually, Pastor Wilkins and the elder tracked the rumors back to their source: a former member of the church and his wife. This disgruntled couple had left the church a year earlier because Pastor Wilkins had confronted the man over some sexual advances he had made to several women in the congregation. Pastor Wilkins had encouraged the man to go through a caring and quiet process of church discipline, combined with counseling with a Christian psychologist. Pastor Wilkins had wanted to help the man, not humiliate him—but the man and his wife had chosen to leave the church instead. He still had many friends in the church, however, and was now using them to inject the venom of his bitterness into the church.

Pastor Wilkins met the problem head-on. He went before his congregation and preached a sermon from Joshua 22 and Matthew 18, a sermon he called, "Don't Rush To Judgment." At the end of the sermon, he publicly confronted the rumors against him and encouraged his people to deal with such questions head-on and face-to-face. Pastor Wilkins and his church are still recovering from the wounds caused by one embittered former parishioner—and by the willingness of a lot of *present* parishioners to rashly judge their own pastor.

In Joshua 22, we see that Israel made a similar mistake—and with similar results. A rash, impetuous judgment brought division and hurt into the community of Israel. It was a dangerous, potentially explosive situation—and civil war threatened the peace of the newly settled and pacified land. But through the providence of God, tragedy was narrowly averted and Israel learned some valuable lessons—lessons that you and I can apply to our own lives some thirty-four centuries later.

The Admonition of Joshua (22:1–8)

The eastern tribes of Reuben, Gad, and the half-tribe of Manasseh had performed well. They were called before Joshua, who commended them for keeping their word to God and for fighting alongside their brothers in the hard struggle for the conquest of Canaan. For seven long years, these men—whose homelands had already been secured and settled *east* of the Jordan—had been separated from wives and families in order to join the fight *west* of the Jordan. Now the battles were over, the land was divided, and it was time to return home.

Joshua dismissed the 40,000 soldiers of the Transjordanian tribes with honor. Recreating this scene, Francis Schaeffer writes,

> If we use a little imagination, we can feel the tremendous emotion involved in the parting of these comrades-at-arms. We can picture the men going through the camp, finding the friends with whom they had fought side by side and saying good-bye to some who had even saved their lives. They shook hands and they parted, as worshipers of God, as friends and fellow companions in war. There is a comradeship among men in titanic moments that is one of the great "mystiques" of life. It is the explanation of the mystique of the rope—two men on a mountain battle nature together, depending for their very lives on a common rope.[1]

As the weary but happy soldiers left, they took with them a substantial share of the spoil taken from the enemy. Joshua had instructed them to share the booty with their brothers who had remained at home.

Why should those who had not endured any of the pain and peril of the conflict enjoy any of the spoil? Some of those who remained behind would no doubt much rather have gone to war, but who then would have raised the crops and protected the women and children? The principle is firmly established that honors and rewards are not to go only to those who carry arms, but also to those who stay home to perform the crucial but less glamorous duties of guarding the home-front.

A Christian businessman recounted a conversation his father had many years ago with a Pullman porter.

> Dad was returning from six weeks of buying wool in Texas. From St. Louis, he took the *Wolverine* to Boston. He had established a good relationship with the porter, and they had several talks together about their mutual faith. The train was pulling out from Back Bay Station, and in a few minutes the trip would be over, and Dad would be at the South Station and a block from his Summer Street office. He was, naturally, excited about getting home and was ready to leave the train, when the porter approached him and said, "Mr. Emery, do you suppose I could ask you a question after my passengers leave?" So Dad remained and after the last passenger disembarked, the porter returned with his question.
>
> "There were two boys in my family. My mother worked very hard to teach us all she could and to see that we had the best education available at that time. I was a good student. When I had graduated from high school, I went to work as a railroad waiter and then I got this job. My whole desire was to help my mother and fulfill her wish that I go to college and become a preacher. She wanted her life to count by seeing her son a preacher. Well, I saved my money and while I was

doing this, my younger brother went in a different direction. He drank and partied and nearly killed himself by living for the devil. About the time I was accepted for college, my brother was converted. He decided he wanted to preach. He had nothing, so he asked me to provide for his education. I was so happy to see this great change in his life that I agreed, and today my brother is a nationally known preacher. You may have heard him on the radio. He has led thousands to Christ. So, you see, I couldn't go into the ministry and I am too old now. Mr. Emery, my question is this: Do you suppose the Lord will give me some credit for the souls my brother led to Him?"

That night, at the dinner table, when my father told this story he was so deeply moved he nearly broke down. We knew what his answer would have been and that the biblical principle is expressed in 1 Samuel 30:24, "For as his share is who goes down to the battle, so shall his share be who stays by the baggage; they shall share alike (RSV)."[2]

The returning soldiers also left with the six solemn exhortations of Joshua ringing in their ears: "But take diligent heed to do the command and the Law . . . to love the Lord your God . . . to walk in all His ways . . . to keep His commandments . . . to cleave unto Him . . . to serve Him with all your heart and all your soul." The charge was short but passionate. Their military obligations were fulfilled, and Joshua was reminding them of their abiding spiritual commitments which were conditions for the continued blessing of God. Like an anxious parent who sees a son or daughter leave home for a place where they could be separated from spiritual influences, so Joshua delivered his earnest charge to the departing warriors. He was fearful that their separation from the rest of the tribes might cause them to drift away from the worship of Jehovah and to embrace idolatry.

The Symbolic Action of the Eastern Tribes (22:9–11)

Leaving Shiloh, the armies of the eastern tribes headed excitedly for home. As they approached the Jordan River, their minds were probably filled with memories of the miraculous crossing seven years before, of the remarkable victory over nearby Jericho, and of the other triumphs shared with their brothers from whom they had so recently separated.

A sense of isolation from the other tribes began to sweep over them. But this was not simply because an ordinary river would separate the eastern from the western tribes, for the Jordan is not an ordinary river. Mountains on each side rise to heights above 2,000 feet and the Jordan valley nestled in between those mountains is like a great trench five to thirteen miles wide. During certain times of the year, the intense heat in that region greatly discourages travelers. This, then, was a very pronounced river boundary and contributed to the fear of these tribesmen that they and their brethren would permanently drift apart. After all, out of sight is often out of mind.

What could be done to keep alive the ties of comradeship forged by the long years of struggle together? What could be done to symbolize the unity between the people on both sides of the river, and to remind everyone in Israel that they were *all* children of the promise? The soldiers from east of the Jordan decided that they should build a huge altar, one that could be seen from a great distance, and which would symbolize their right to worship at the original altar at the tabernacle in Shiloh.

So such an altar was erected on the western side of the Jordan River, so that it could be seen from the eastern shore. Why did they not build some other kind of monument? Because they knew that the true basis of their unity was their common worship, which was centered in the sacrifices at the altar.

The Threat of War (22:12–20)

Unfortunately, this symbol of unity was misconstrued to be a symbol of apostasy. In effect, this intended sign of unity actually became the source of division! When word reached the other tribes, they gathered at Shiloh, the site of the one true altar, and prepared to go to war against the armies of the eastern tribes. On the basis of what they had heard, the Israelites concluded that the eastern tribes were guilty of rebellion against God. They thought that their eastern brothers had set up a second altar of sacrifice, contrary to the Law of Moses (see Lev. 17:8–9). As Francis Schaeffer writes,

> They thought the holiness of God was being threatened. So these men, who were sick of war, said, "The holiness of God demands no compromise." I would to God that the church of the twentieth century would learn this lesson. The holiness of the God who exists demands that there be no compromise in the area of truth.[3]

We must say this in defense of the western tribes: they would not compromise the true worship of God. Yes, they rushed to judgment—but they were zealous for God's honor and truth. Unlike so many Christians today, truth was one area they were not willing to compromise.

Today, compromise is rampant in the Christian church. The late Professor Addison Leitch told of two students in one seminary who were instructed in certain classes not to use the Bible as a support for the positions they took. When one student argued from Scripture, he was ridiculed by both the other students and by the professor. In church after church, seminary after seminary, there are ordained ministers and professors of religion who openly deny the deity of Jesus Christ and other essentials of the faith, yet who serve in their positions unchallenged. Absolute standards have fallen, compromise is applauded, people with strong values are derided as "rigid" and "narrow minded." Today—as in the time of the Judges—everyone does what is right in his own eyes.

Faced with a case of seeming disobedience and disregard for God's commands, the western tribes of Israel called for a war of judgment and purification against their eastern brothers. And though we can admire the zeal for the truth and purity of worship that is displayed here, we can only feel relieved that wisdom prevailed over their initial rash judgment. They ultimately decided to talk first rather than fight with the two and one-half tribes of the east. In this way, they hoped to persuade their brothers to abandon their project and avoid war.

When Charles Haddon Spurgeon was a boy, he asked his mother for some eggs from her chickens. She answered, "You may have them if you pay for them." Someone overheard and circulated rumors that the Spurgeons were so petty and miserly that they made their children pay for eggs, milk, and butter. At Mrs. Spurgeon's death, the explanation came out, when books recording profits from all sales were found with the note that all these profits were devoted to the support of two elderly widows of Welsh ministers.

It is dangerous and unwise to act on suspicion without proof. It is sin and foolishness to judge people's motives on the basis of circumstantial evidence alone. It is rank disobedience to God's Word to spread damaging rumors about other people. Among the sins listed in Proverbs 6 as "abominations" which "the Lord hates" are, "A false witness who utters lies, and one who spreads strife among brothers."[4]

Phinehas, noted for his righteous zeal for the Lord (see Num. 25:6–18), headed a deputation of ten tribal rulers whose responsibility was to confront the others. Arriving at the scene of the new altar, the appointed group charged the eastern tribesmen with unheard of wickedness, characterizing their action as a trespass, iniquity, and rebellion. They reminded the eastern tribes that the iniquity of Peor brought God's judgment on the whole nation (see Num. 25), as did the sin of Achan (Josh. 7). Now the entire congregation was in jeopardy once again because of this alleged act of rebellion.

Then Phinehas magnanimously suggested that if the eastern tribes felt that the land east of Jordan was unclean—that is, if they felt it was not hallowed by God's presence—the western tribes would make room for them on their side of the Jordan. This was a generous, loving offer, involving material cost. As Schaeffer observes,

> Once more, here is the tragedy of the modern church! Our spirituality and our brotherhood often stop at the point of material possessions. In the early church this was not so. The Christians had things in common not because there was a law to this effect, not because this was an enforced Marx-Engels communism, but because they loved each other. And a love that does not go down into the practical stuff of life, including money and possessions, is absolute junk! To think that love is talking softly rather than saying something sharply and that is not carried down into the practical stuff of life is not biblical. We must say with tears that the evangelical church in our generation has been poor at this point.[5]

The Defense of the Eastern Tribes
(22:21–29)

The Israelite delegation was about to learn how wrong their rash judgments and stern denunciations had been. The facts behind the construction of the altar by the Jordan now came to light.

Instead of responding to the fierce reproof in anger, the eastern tribes in candor and sincerity solemnly repudiated the charge that they in fact erected a rival altar in rebellion against God. Invoking God as a witness they swore twice by His three names—El, Elohim, Jehovah (the Mighty One, God, the Lord)—affirming that if their act was in rebellion against God and His commands, then they deserved His judgment.

Why then was the second altar built? They explained that it was occasioned by the geographic separation of their people and the effect this separation might have on future generations. In verses 24 and 25, they replied:

In time to come your sons may say to our sons, "What have you to do with the Lord, the God of Israel? For the Lord has made the Jordan a border between us and you, you sons of Reuben and sons of Gad; you have no portion in the Lord." So your sons may make our sons stop fearing the Lord.

The eastern tribesman made it clear that they were fully aware of God's laws governing Israel's worship; their recently erected altar was not intended as a place for sacrifices and offerings, but as a witness to all generations that the Transjordanian tribes had a right to cross the Jordan and worship at Shiloh. This altar was only a copy of the true worship center and an evidence of their right to visit and worship at the original altar.

While we must deeply admire their concern for the spiritual welfare of future generations it would appear that the action of the two and one-half tribes was unnecessary. God had ordained in the Law that all Israelite males were to appear at the sanctuary three times a year. (See Ex. 23:17.) This, if heeded, would have preserved the unity of the tribes, both spiritually and politically.

The building of another altar was also a dangerous precedent. John J. Davis comments,

> The unifying factor in ancient Israel was not her culture, architecture, economy, or even military objectives. The long-range unifying factor was her worship of Jehovah. When the central sanctuary was abandoned as the true place of worship, the tribes then developed independent sanctuaries, thus alienating themselves from other tribes and weakening their military potential. The effects of this trend are fully seen in the period of the Judges.[6]

The Reconciliation of the Tribes (22:30–34)

There was a happy ending to this grave crisis as the explanation of the eastern tribes was fully accepted by Phinehas and his delegation, as well as by the other tribes. In concluding the entire matter, Phinehas expressed deep gratitude that no sin had been committed and that the wrath of God therefore was not incurred.

In a book describing the occupation and distribution of the Promised Land, why should this single incident be treated in such detail? Simply because it illustrates certain principles that were vital to the Israelites living harmoniously together in the land and under God's full blessing.

In Joshua chapter 22, we discover four principles that are just as applicable today as they were in Joshua's day—principles that all of us as Christian leaders would do well to build into our lives:

• *Never compromise God's truth.* Be zealous for the purity of the faith. There is always a price to pay when we surrender our convictions. In Jude 3, the apostle urges his readers to "contend earnestly for the faith which was once for all delivered to the saints."

Yet, in our zeal, we should also remember:

• *Never judge other people's motives on the basis of circumstantial evidence.* We need to gather all the facts—not form hasty judgments on the basis of an emotionally charged account of a situation. "He who gives an answer before he hears," says Proverbs 18:13, "it is folly and shame to him."

• *Discuss controversies frankly, openly, and humbly in order to clear the air and reach reconciliation.* Such confrontations must be conducted in a spirit of meekness, not spiritual superiority. "If your brother sins," said Jesus, "go and reprove him in private; if he listens to you, you have won your brother."[7] And Paul adds, "Brethren, even if a man is caught in any trespass, you who are spiritual, restore such a one in a spirit of gentleness, looking to yourself, lest you too be tempted."[8]

• *If wrongly accused, respond calmly and gently, praying for God's help to respond in a way that is both honoring to Him and empowered by Him.* Here, the wise counsel of Solomon is indispensable: "A gentle answer turns away wrath, but a harsh word stirs up anger."[9]

These principles will save us from many an error and needless battle—and they will guide us safely through those crises of conflict which inevitably arise to test our leadership skills. May God make of us Christian leaders who not only speak the truth without compromise, but who *seek* the truth without bias or prejudice. May He make of us people who judge rightly, not rashly. May He make of us people who fearlessly confront sin and error—but who confront sin and error in ourselves before we look for it in others.

That is the delicate but crucial balance God calls us to find as we live every day for Him.

QUESTIONS FOR REFLECTION AND DISCUSSION

See Your Own Reflection

1. How do you usually respond when you are misjudged or misunderstood? Do you angrily defend yourself? Fight back? Withdraw? Pray? Respond calmly?

Dig a Little Deeper

2. How were the two and one-half tribes east of the Jordan different from the rest of Israel?

These eastern or Transjordanian tribes had just sacrificed greatly in order to help the western tribes conquer Canaan. On their way home from the wars, the eastern tribes erected an altar as a reminder of their right to worship at the true altar in Shiloh. As a result, the western Israelites flew off the handle and were ready to go to war against the very brothers who had just helped them win their own land! Who do you think was more responsible for this misunderstanding? The Israelites east of the Jordan, or the Israelites west of the Jordan? Explain.

3. Read verse 17 and Numbers 25. What was the sin of Peor? Were the western Israelites justified in comparing the second altar at the Jordan to the sins of Peor and Achan? Or were they over-reacting?

4. Who was Phinehas? Why do you suppose he was chosen to lead the delegation to the eastern tribes? What qualities in Phinehas do you admire?

How did Phinehas and the rest of Israel respond when the eastern tribes explained themselves? What would have happened had they responded differently?

Let's Get Personal

6. Share a time when you rashly and wrongly judged another person.

Which of the four principles at the end of this chapter would have helped you to avoid this error?

What else might you have done differently to avoid the error of misjudging another person's motives?

7. Joshua 22 opens with a scene of partings and leave-takings between comrades-in-arms. Who have you had to say good-bye to during the past year?

Is there a parting or leave-taking coming soon in your life? Who is the person you need to say good-bye to? What else do you feel God is calling you to say to that person?

12

THE COUNSEL OF AN OLD SOLDIER

JOSHUA 23–24

On April 19, 1951, an old soldier said farewell.

Having been relieved of his duties by President Truman, General Douglas MacArthur appeared before Congress and said,

> The world has turned over many times since I took the oath on the plain at West Point, and the hopes and dreams have long since vanished. But I still remember the refrain of one of the most popular barracks ballads of that day which proclaimed proudly that old soldiers never die; they just fade away. And like the old soldier in that ballad, I now close my military career and just fade away, an old soldier who tried to do his duty as God gave him the sight to see that duty.

The book of Joshua ends on just such a note: an old soldier bids farewell, just before he fades away into history. His parting words are tinged with sadness, like all last words. And they express Joshua's deep concern for his beloved nation, Israel. He is troubled by the growing complacency he sees—a willingness on the part of the Israelites to compromise and co-exist with the last remaining Canaanites. God did not intend Israel to share the land with the Canaanites; he intended it to be the exclusive domain of Israel.

With Israel's enemies practically vanquished, Joshua knew well the danger of his people letting down their moral guard. Before his departure from active leadership, he felt compelled to warn his fledgling nation of the moral and spiritual dangers that still surrounded them.

Over two-hundred years ago, an American scholar named Alexander Tyler pronounced a similar warning to his own fledgling nation—the United States of America, which was then less than ten years old. Like Joshua before him, Tyler foresaw the moral and spiritual dangers that come with success, prosperity, and complacency. So he wrote these words—words which now read more like an epitaph than a warning:

> The average age of the world's greatest civilizations has been two-hundred years. These nations have progressed through this sequence: From bondage to spiritual faith; from spiritual faith to great courage; from courage to liberty; from liberty to abundance; from abundance to complacency; from complacency to apathy; from apathy to dependency; from dependency again into bondage.

Tyler knew, as did Joshua, that continued obedience to God's commands was essential to continued enjoyment of His blessings. The story of Israel in the days of Joshua was never more timely and urgent than it is right now, as we see our own nation sliding back toward the bondage Alexander Tyler foresaw.

Joshua's Final Challenge to the Leaders (23:1–16)

Although some have suggested that in these final chapters we have two reports of the same event, it seems best to view chapter 23 as Joshua's challenge to Israel's leaders, and chapter 24 as his charge to Israel's people. We will begin by examining Joshua's challenge to the leaders, which Joshua delivered in three segments or cycles.

The scene of Joshua's speech was probably Shiloh, where the tabernacle was located. It was some fifteen or twenty years after the end of the conquest and distribution of the land when Joshua summoned Israel's leaders so that he could encourage, exhort, and warn them of the dangers of departing from the true worship of Jehovah. It was a solemn and historic occasion. Those in attendance included the elders, family heads, judges, officers, and soldiers of conquest (who had now exchanged their swords for plowshares). Doubtless Caleb and Phinehas were there as well.

The leaders of Israel came, eagerly and without hesitation, to hear the parting words of their most honored and admired citizen. This veteran commander wanted to speak on one theme: God's unfailing faithfulness to Israel, and Israel's corresponding duty to be faithful to God. Three times he repeated his central message. Three times he emphasized the faithfulness of God and the responsibility of Israel. He undoubtedly triple-underscored this message because he wanted to make triple-sure that Israel would hear it and heed it.

1. The First Cycle (verses 3–8).

Avoiding any temptation to elevate himself, Joshua reminded the leaders of Israel that their enemies had been defeated solely because the Lord God had fought for them. The battles and the victories were not theirs, but God's. The psalmist reiterated this affirmation: "For by their own sword they did not possess the land; and their own arm did not save them; but Thy right hand, and Thine arm, and the light of Thy presence, for Thou didst favor them."[1] As for the Canaanites who still lingered about the country, the Lord God would drive them out also so that Israel could inherit the land they occupied.

Seeking to impress the Israelites with their responsibility, Joshua passed on the very words Jehovah had armed him with—just as Jehovah had directly instructed Joshua when it was time to cross over the Jordan. Courage and obedience, the ingredients which were so necessary to the successful conquest of Canaan, were just as essential now.

Joshua's worst nightmare was that, after all of Israel's successes on the battlefield, Israel might ultimately lose the war by becoming conformed to the heathen nations around them. He forbade all contact and intimacy with the Canaanite enemy. Joshua foresaw the perilous path ahead of Israel: the people would backslide, inch by inch and step by step until at last—before they even realized how far they had sunk—God's people would be prostrating themselves before the shrines of pagan deities.

Spiritual compromise is a gradual and deceptive process. It is going on all around us—and perhaps even within us—today. In fact, spiritual compromise has been a problem for the Christian church since the very beginning. In the early church, some Christians made their living by carving and gilding images of pagan gods for sale to the Greeks and Romans. Since they did not worship these gods nor bow in their shrines, these Christians saw no harm in producing and polishing such images for sale. Their reasoning was, "After all, somebody will do it anyway—and I have to live." But Tertullian, the Christian apologist, replied, *"Must* you live?"

Joshua and Tertullian joined in affirming that a believer has only one *"must,"* and that is to be faithful to the Lord.

2. The Second Cycle (verses 9–13).

Returning to his theme, Joshua again affirmed God's past faithfulness to Israel. Jehovah fought their battles for them, and while some of the Canaanites did indeed remain in the land, wherever an enemy had been encountered he had been overcome.

Israel was then solemnly exhorted, on the basis of divine interventions on their behalf, to *love God.* Maintaining love for God would require diligence and watchfulness on the part of the Israelites, because of the proximity of their corrupt neighbors. The temptation would be strong to gradually forsake Jehovah and absorb the attitudes and ways of the Canaanites—a choice that would be fatal to the nation of Israel. This danger is graphically described by Joshua in terms of the dire results that would follow:

• God would no longer drive out these heathen people, but they would remain to mar Israel's inheritance.

• The Canaanites who remained among them would be as snares and traps to entangle them, as scourges to lash them, and as thorns that fly back into the face, stabbing the eyes.

• Miseries and troubles would increase for Israel until, finally and tragically, the people of Israel would be dispossessed from their land.

Joshua did not contemplate any possibility of neutrality as he posed the choice to be made: either Israel's

God—or the gods and values of Canaan. Joshua's day was no time for neutrality. And today is no time for neutrality either. As Jesus Himself has said, "No one can serve two masters."[2]

In one of his fables, Aesop told of the time when the beasts and birds were engaged in war. The bat tried to belong to both parties. When the birds were victorious, he would fly around announcing that he was a bird. But when the beasts won a fight, he would assure everyone that he was a beast. Soon his hypocrisy was discovered and he was rejected by both the beasts and the birds. Today, as a result, the bat can appear only at night.

Like the bat, Israel was destined for misery if its people did not choose, firmly and decisively, in favor of the right master. Failure to heed Joshua's warning would one day extract a bitter price from the people of Israel. "Like the spotted leopard, with its graceful form and gentle gait," writes G. W. Butler, "so is the faltering, fawning world. Who would suspect danger? But cleave thereunto, and ere long its strength and cruelty will appear, and its miserable victims will be torn to pieces in its teeth and talons."[3]

3. The Third Cycle (verses 14–16).

Like a masterful preacher, Joshua recapped his discourse, this time as a dying man, in the hope that his words would sink more deeply into their hearts. Once more he spoke of God's absolute faithfulness to every promise. Once more he warned of the doom of the disobedient.

Joshua's anxiety concerned the Canaanite remnant. As this old soldier looked into the future, he foresaw Israel's sinful compromise with the alien gods of Canaan, and he prophesied a tragic fate that would inevitably overtake the people of God when they violated the covenant God had made with them.

The terrible and sobering climax of Joshua's message to the leaders emphasized the fact that Israel's greatest danger was not a military threat from the outside. It was a moral and spiritual threat from within. And if Joshua were alive today, he would likely give the same warnings to us today.

Our nation—and indeed our entire civilization—now faces a grave danger. The collapse of Communism and the dismantling of the Berlin Wall, along with the intimidation or outright defeat of international bullies such as Saddam Hussein and Muammar Qaddafi, may present an illusion that the world is a kinder, gentler, safer place. *But it is not.* America continues to occupy an insecure place in a hostile world—but as in Joshua's Israel, the gravest danger we face is not a military threat from without, but a moral and spiritual threat from within.

As a culture, and as individuals, we have been mesmerized by the myth of progress—the idea that things always have a way of getting better with the passage of time. To this myth, Dr. Gerhard Schroeder, then West German Federal Minister of the Interior, replied in a 1954 address:

> It was the stimulating conviction of our grandfathers that civilization on the basis of *technical progress was bound to lead to permanent improvement* of the world and *finally to a happy solution of all its problems.*
>
> A few thinkers tried to criticize this optimism as naive. Today they seem to us great prophets who anticipated the present crisis.
>
> More and more, philosophers, historians, and poets of the different nations have pointed out that *belief in the progress of the world is an error.*

The political events, the social revolutions, and the confusion of philosophical thought at the present time have *confirmed these pessimistic prophecies.* The optimism of the past has turned into *dark pessimism!*

To these words, Dr. Richard Halverson adds his commentary:

Experience has served to confirm the "dark pessimism."

Not only are we not solving our human problems— *they are compounding* . . . crime, drug abuse, alcoholism, divorce, terrorism, child abuse, wife abuse, etc.

We have become *technological giants* . . . and *moral adolescents.*

Our progress in ethics and morals and humanness has declined in *inverse ratio* to our technical and scientific expertise.[4]

Joshua's Final Charge to the People (24:1–28)

Joshua's last meeting with the people took place at Shechem. Whether this second gathering occurred soon after the previous one, whether it was held on an anniversary of Joshua's earlier address, or whether it was after a long interval, cannot be determined from the text.

The geographical setting is of interest. Shechem, located a few miles northwest of Shiloh, was the place where Abraham first received the promise that God would give his seed the land of Canaan. Abraham responded by building an altar to demonstrate his faith in the one true God. (See Gen. 12:6–7.)

Jacob, too, stopped at Shechem on his return from Padan-aram and buried there the idols his family had brought with them. (See Gen. 35:4.) When the Israelites completed the first phase of the conquest of Canaan, they journeyed to Shechem where Joshua built an altar to Jehovah, inscribed the Law of God on stone pillars, and reviewed these laws for all the people (Josh. 8:30–35.)

There was good reason, therefore, for Joshua to convene the Israelites at this location. Certainly the stones on which the Law had been written were still standing, vivid reminders of that significant event. But from this moment on, the beautiful valley between Mt. Ebal and Mt. Gerizim would be associated with this poignant farewell scene, as their honored leader spoke to them for the last time, perhaps with an old and quavering voice.

The literary form of this discourse has occasioned a great deal of interest and comment as well. We now known that the rulers of the Hittite Empire in this period (1450–1200 B.C.) established international agreements with their vassal states, obligating them to serve the king in faithfulness and obedience. These suzerainty[5] treaties followed a regular pattern and required periodic renewal.

It seems clear that in Joshua 24 we have, in the standard suzerainty treaty form of the time, a covenant renewal document in which the people of Israel were called upon to confirm their covenant relationship with their God. The Mosaic Covenant established at Sinai was not an everlasting covenant. It had to renewed in every generation. That renewal was now transacted in a formal and impressive ceremony.

1. Reviewing Their Blessings (verses 1–13).

The opening two verses identify the Lord God as Author of the Covenant and Israel as the vassal nation. Following this preamble is the historical prologue, reviewing God's past blessing upon His subjects. He brought them out of Ur of the Chaldees, out of Egypt, and into Canaan.

It was God who speaks in this recapitulation of Israel's history. No less than seventeen times the personal pronoun "I" is used—"I took . . . I gave . . . I sent . . . I plagued . . . I brought . . . I delivered." Any greatness Israel achieved was not by the effort of the Israelite people, but through God's grace and power. From first to last, Israel's conquests, deliverances, and prosperity were due to the good mercies of God, not their own strength.

Is this not what every believer is forced to acknowledge? All that we are and have has come by God's grace—and we owe it all to Him.

John Newton, the slave trader who found Christ in the middle of the stormy seas, wrote a text in large letters and hung it above his mantelpiece as a constant reminder: "Thou shalt remember that thou wast a bondman in the land of Egypt, and the Lord thy God redeemed thee."[6] As Francis Schaeffer makes clear,

> Whether studying the Old Testament or the New, we are reminded that we are not where we are because of a long, wise, and godly heritage. We come from rebellion. Individually, we are children of wrath. After we are Christians, we must look at others who are still under God's wrath and always say, "I am essentially what you are. If I am in a different place, it is not because I am intrinsically better than you, but simply because God has done something in my life." There is no place for pride.[7]

2. Rehearsing Their Responsibilities (verses 14–24).

Joshua then stated what the terms of the covenant renewal would be: Israel must fear Jehovah and serve Him. Again, we see a parallel with the treaties of the Hittites. In the Hittite treaties, foreign alliances were prohibited. In God's covenant, Israel was to reject alliances with foreign gods. Joshua boldly challenged them to choose between the gods of Ur (which their ancestors worshiped), the gods of their old slavemasters in Egypt, the gods of their enemies, the Amorites—or *the one true God, Jehovah.*

Then, in verse 15, Joshua adds example to exhortation, assuring the people that whatever their choice, *his* mind was made up, *his* course was clear: "As for me and my house, we will serve the Lord."

The people responded eagerly, moved by the force of Joshua's arguments and the magnetism of his personal example. They despised the very thought of forsaking the God who had delivered them out of Egypt, protected them in the wilderness, and brought them into the land of promise. "Far be it from us," they proclaimed in verse 16, "that we should forsake the Lord to serve other gods."

Joshua spoke a second time. He was not at all satisfied with their spontaneous burst of enthusiasm. Did he detect some traces of insincerity? Had he hoped that the people would bring forth their idols for destruction, as Jacob's family had done in this same place, centuries before? There was no such response. Whatever his reasons, Joshua saw fit to drive the point home yet again. In verses 19 and 20, he bluntly declared, "You will not be able to serve the Lord, for He is a holy God. He is a jealous God; He will not forgive your transgression or your sins. If you forsake the Lord and serve foreign gods, then He will turn and do you harm and consume you after He has done good to you."

Of course, Joshua did not mean that God is not a God of forgiveness. He meant that God is not to be worshiped nor served lightly, and that to deliberately forsake Him to serve idols would be presumptuous, willful sin with severe consequences under the Law. (See Num. 15:30.) Once again, the people responded to Joshua's tough words, resoundingly affirming their intense desire to serve Jehovah.

Then Joshua spoke a third time, pointedly challenging them to serve as witnesses against themselves if they ever fell away from God. And the people immediately replied, verse 22, "We are witnesses."

In verse 23, Joshua spoke a fourth and final time, coming to the point he had been building toward: "Now therefore, put away the foreign gods which are in your midst." He had heard the pledge from their lips. Now he challenged them to prove their sincerity by their works. Knowing that many of them were secretly practicing idolatry, Joshua forthrightly demanded that they remove and destroy the foreign gods. Without the slightest hesitation the people shouted, verse 24, "We will serve the Lord our God, and will obey His voice."

There could be no mixing of allegiance to God with idol worship. A firm choice had to be made then, as in every generation. People must choose between expediency and principle, between this world and eternity, between God and idols. You may protest, "But this issue has nothing to do with me! I don't worship idols!" To this sentiment, Joy Davidson replies,

> What shape is an idol? I worship Ganesa, brother, god of worldly wisdom, patron of shopkeepers. He is in the shape of a little fat man with an elephant's head; he is made of soapstone and has two small rubies for eyes. What shape do you worship?
>
> I worship a fishtail Cadillac convertible, brother. All my days I give it offerings of oil and polish. Hours of

my time are devoted to its ritual; and it brings me luck in all my undertakings; and it establishes me among my fellows as a success in life. What model is your car, brother?

I worship my house beautiful, sister. Long and loving meditation have I spent on it; the chairs contrast with the rug, the curtains harmonize with the woodwork, all of it is perfect and holy. The ashtrays are in exactly the right places, and should some blasphemer drop ashes on the floor, I nearly die of shock. I live only for the service of my house, and it rewards me with the envy of my sisters, who must rise up and call me blessed. Lest my children profane the holiness of my house with dirt and noise, I drive them out-of-doors. What shape is your idol, sister? Is it your house, or your clothes, or perhaps even your worthwhile and cultural club?

I worship the pictures I paint, brother. . . . I worship my job. . . . I worship my golf game. . . . I worship my comfort; after all, isn't enjoyment the goal of life? I worship my church; I want to tell you, the work we've done in missions beats all other denominations in this city, and next year we can afford that new organ, and you won't find a better choir anywhere. . . .
What shape is your idol?[8]

3. *The Reminders of Their Pledge (verses 25–28).*

Realizing that further words would be fruitless, satisfied with the genuineness and sincerity of the people's consecration, Joshua solemnly renewed the covenant. In verse 26, he proceeded to write down the agreement "in the Book of the Law of God." This was then placed beside the Ark of the Covenant. (See Deut. 31:24–27.) Again, this is a parallel to Hittite practice, for among the Hittites, the suzerainty treaty was placed in the sanctuary of worship of the vassal nation.

As a final reminder, Joshua apparently inscribed the terms of the covenant, which the people had just publicly reaffirmed, onto a large stone slab, which was set up beneath the oak belonging to this sacred location. Archaeologists excavating the site of Shechem have uncovered a great limestone pillar which may be identified with the memorial referred to here. Joshua declared the inscribed stone to be a witness, as if the stone had heard all of the transactions of the covenant, and declared its witness through the inscription he had placed upon it.

As he led the people of Israel in a sacred ritual of covenant renewal—a ritual in which the people pledged to honor, fear, and follow the Lord God—Joshua completed his last public act. With the memories of this solemn occasion indelibly impressed on their minds, the Israelites returned to their homes in possession of their inheritance.

Planting for Eternity

Like the apostle Paul who came centuries later, Joshua had finished his course. He had kept the faith. His last act was to look beyond the present moment, to peer into the future, to once again bring his people together and mold them into a unified moral and spiritual community, and to prepare them for the perils and challenges to come. In his last official act, we find a final "secret" of godly leadership embedded in the life and the example of Joshua: *A true Christian leader looks not only to the present, but to the future. He builds not only for his own lifetime, but for eternity.*

The leadership model of the book of Joshua has come full circle. At the beginning of the book, Moses had just died and Joshua had just emerged from the shadow of that late, great leader after decades of being mentored by him. By the end of the book, Joshua was old and death was about to claim him, just as it claimed Moses before him. So he did what he could to put steel in the backbones of his people, to challenge them, to encourage them, to confront them with the solemn responsibility and the dangerous world in which he would leave them.

There is an old Chinese proverb which expresses the view of Israel's history that Joshua took as he was about to bid farewell to the world:

> If you are planting for a year, plant grain.
> If you are planting for a decade, plant trees.
> If you are planting for a century, plant people.

Joshua was looking even beyond the next century. He was looking down the millennia as he sought to plant his people firmly in their land and in their faith. He was taking not only the long view, but the *eternal* view. Time would tell if these people, with their resounding declarations of faith and loyalty to their God, would stay planted for the next one hundred or one thousand years. But Joshua had done all he could do to help their faith and fidelity to take root and flourish. The rest was up to the people themselves.

Joshua's time among them was over.

Three Peaceful Graves (24:29–33)

Three burials mark the close of the book of Joshua. The first burial is Joshua's. It is recorded that Joshua died at the age of 110 years and was buried in his own town. No greater tribute could be paid to this man than the fact that he was called simply "the servant of the Lord." He aspired to no greater rank than this. The sacred historian of the book of Joshua also took note of the high esteem in which Joshua was held at the time of his death, verse 31: "And Israel served the Lord all the days of Joshua and all the days of the elders who survived Joshua."

What a contrast is seen between those words and the words of a noted British historian who said recently of certain contemporary leaders, "They are men who cannot control their passions, keep their wives faithful to themselves, or their sons out of brothels—and we look to them to control international tempers and preserve peace!"

The second burial is that of the bones of Joseph. Joseph's dying request was that he be buried in the Promised Land. Now, after the long years of the wanderings and the conquest, his remains were laid to rest in a field in Shechem that once belonged to his father Jacob. Another circle was closed. Joseph—who had not been in Canaan since he was sold into slavery by his brothers—had come home at last.

The third burial was that of the high priest Eleazar, son and successor of Aaron. It was his privilege to be associated with Joshua in the distribution of the land (see Num. 34:17), and to direct the ministry of tabernacle worship in the crucial years of the conquest and settlement of Canaan.

These three tranquil graves testify to the faithfulness of God. All three of these great men—Joshua, Joseph, and Eleazar—had once lived as exiles in foreign lands, but they had all returned home to Canaan. All three had found their final resting place within the borders of the Promised Land. God kept His Word to Joshua, Joseph, Eleazar—and to all Israel. Just as these great leaders of Israel could count on the unfailing faithfulness of God, so can you and I. As we hear in the words of that great hymn by William M. Runyon,

Great is Thy faithfulness, O God my Father,
There is no shadow of turning with Thee;
Thou changest not, Thy compassions, they fail not;
As Thou has been Thou forever wilt be.

Great is Thy faithfulness! Great is Thy faithfulness!
Morning by morning new mercies I see;
All I have needed Thy hand hath provided—
Great is thy faithfulness, Lord, unto me!

QUESTIONS FOR REFLECTION AND DISCUSSION

See Your Own Reflection

1. In this passage, the veteran soldier, Joshua, gives the people and the leaders of Israel his final words of advice and counsel before he "fades away" into eternity. Looking back over your own life, what is the best advice you have ever received?

If you were going to die tomorrow, what one piece of advice and counsel would you give to the people you leave behind?

Dig a Little Deeper

2. Read 23:3–5. What does Joshua remind the Israelite leaders of in this passage? Why is this reminder important?

Read 23:9–11. What is the result of love, loyalty, and obedience toward God?

3. Read 23:12–13. What are the signs—and the results—of falling away from God?

4. In 23:14–16, Joshua seems to present God as Someone who makes good on His promises—and on His threats! Is our God a "threatening" God? Is the God of Joshua the same God who is presented in the New Testament?

5. Has your study of God's actions on behalf of Israel in the days of Joshua *changed* your impression of who God is and what He is like? What truths about God's nature and character have you learned from this study that you can apply in your own life?

6. Read 24:1 and compare with Gen. 12:6–7 and 33:18–20. Why do you think Joshua chose Shechem as the place to assemble the people for his final address?

7. In verse 2 through 15, Joshua recounts all that God has done for Israel, then calls for a response from

the people. What is Joshua's challenge to Israel? What does Joshua say he and his family will do?

How do the people respond to his challenge? Why does Joshua not seem to fully accept or believe their response?

If you made the same response as the people of Israel did, would Joshua be just as dubious about your claim to faithfulness to God?

How can we, as Christians at the end of the twentieth century, show that we are sincere about our faith and loyalty to the Lord?

Let's Get Personal

8. Reread Joshua 24:23–24 and the quote in this chapter by Joy Davidson. Look honestly within yourself. What are your idols?

Are you willing to throw away your idols and yield your heart completely to God? Why or why not?

9. Read the "epitaph" of Joshua, 24:31. What would you like your epitaph to be when you die? Are you in the process of "writing" that epitaph with your life right now? Why or why not?

What is the one thing you want to be remembered for after you "fade away" from history?

Appendix

JOSHUA'S SECRETS OF LEADERSHIP

Throughout this study in the life and times of Joshua, we have discerned fifteen "secrets" of godly leadership embedded in the example left to us by this great man of God. We have collected these "secrets" in this appendix for ready reference. We hope you will be encouraged to go back to the example of Joshua again and again for insight and inspiration as you seek to be the kind of strong, courageous, faithful Christian leader God wants you to be.

DISCOVERY HOUSE PUBLISHERS

❏ A true Christian leader maintains continual fellowship with God—not only in public, but in private, where nobody else sees. He talks to God. He listens to God. He searches God's Word for insight and guidance.

❏ A true Christian leader trusts and obeys God, expecting Him to do the impossible. By faith, a true Christian leader steps out into the river of impossibility, knowing that nothing is impossible with God.

❏ A leader does not allow himself to be pressured or rushed into hasty action. If you feel pressured to make a decision or to take action prematurely, *stop!* Resist that pressure. Consult with the Lord. Seek wise counsel from other Christians. God does not require you to make major decisions without adequate opportunity for prayer and consideration.

❏ Consecration precedes conquest. Whatever task you undertake, prepare yourself mentally, physically, emotionally, and spiritually for that task. Then pour everything you have into that task, and carry it out with complete singleness of mind.

❏ Whatever your leadership role, acknowledge God as your Commander-in-Chief. The battle is His, not yours. He will fight your battles for you—if you allow Him to do so.

❏ A true Christian leader must be able to take orders as well as give them. Those who cannot obey are not qualified to lead. And the One whose orders are to be obeyed above all others, without questioning or hesitation, is God Himself.

❏ Never compromise or flirt with sin. Compromise with evil will destroy a Christian leader. It will create disaster in your spiritual life, your relationships, your business life, and your ministry. It will ruin your reputation. It will affect the behavior and infect the faith of people around you. Sin is a deadly disease and it is extremely contagious. Wherever you find sin in your life, root it out, destroy it, deal with it fully and decisively.

❏ Never underestimate the enemy or overestimate yourself.

❏ A true Christian leader keeps commitments. God honors us when we honor our commitments—even commitments we have entered into foolishly or which we have been tricked into, and even commitments which are costly to us. God honors the Christian leader who is reliable and dependable, and whose word can be trusted.

❏ A true Christian leader is persistent. He perseveres to the end. He never gives up.

❏ A Christian leader never compromises God's truth. Be zealous for the purity of the faith. There is always a price to pay when we surrender our convictions.

❏ Never judge other people's motives or prejudge a case on the grounds of circumstantial evidence. Gather all the facts. Avoid forming hasty judgments on the basis of an emotionally charged account of a situation.

❏ Discuss controversies frankly, openly, and humbly in order to clear the air and reach reconciliation. Such confrontations must be conducted in a spirit of meekness, not spiritual superiority.

❏ If wrongly accused, respond calmly and gently, praying for God's help to respond in a way that is both honoring to Him and empowered by Him. Here, the wise counsel of Proverbs 15:1 is indispensable: "A gentle answer turns away wrath, but a harsh word stirs up anger."

❏ A true Christian leader looks not only to the present, but to the future. He builds not only for his own lifetime, but for eternity.

NOTES

Chapter 1: Filling the Leadership Vacuum

1. Max DePree, *Leadership is an Art* (Dell, p. 14).

2. William S. LaSor, *Great Personalities of the Bible* (Revell, p. 77).

3. Francis Schaeffer, *How Should We Then Live?* (Revell, p. 226).

4. Alan Redpath, *Victorious Christian Living* (Revell, pp. 32–33).

5. Harold F. Boss, *How Green Was My Grazing* (Taylor Publishing Co., p. 272).

Chapter 2: Living in Enemy Territory

1. George Hague, *Practical Studies in the History and Biography of the Old Testament* (Witness Printing House, p. 11).

2. William Blaikie, *The Book of Joshua* (Hodder & Stoughton, p. 85).

3. Erwin Lutzer, *The Morality Gap* (Moody Press, p. 55).

4. Heb. 11:6,31.

5. Francis A. Schaeffer, *Joshua and the Flow of Biblical History* (InterVarsity Press, pp. 79–80).

Chapter 3: The River of Impossibility

1. Robert Hemfelt, Frank Minirth, and Paul Meier, *Love is a Choice* (Thomas Nelson Publishers, pp. 13–14).

2. John J. Davis, *Conquest and Crisis* (Baker, p. 35).

3. Psalm 27:3 (KJV).

4. Deut. 6:6–7.

5. Alexander Maclaren, *Expositions of Holy Scripture*, III, p. 122.

Chapter 5: God's Strategy for Victory

1. Psalm 24:9 (KJV).
2. Alexander Maclaren, *Expositions of Holy Scripture*, III, p. 136.
3. Gleason Archer, *A Survey of Old Testament Introduction* (Moody Press, p. 261).
4. Heb. 11:30.
5. *Bible Knowledge*, March 1972, p. 45.
6. Richard Halverson, *Perspective*, May 10, 1978.

Chapter 6: The Agony of Defeat

1. Alexander Whyte, *Bible Characters*, First Series, Zondervan, p. 292.
2. Mark H. McCormack *What They Don't Teach You at Harvard Business School: Notes From a Street-Smart Executive* (Bantam Books, p. 205).
3. Matt. 10:16.
4. Eph. 6:10.
5. Num. 14:2–3.
6. Wesley G. Hunt, "Sin in the Camp," *The Sunday School Times and Gospel Herald*, November 15, 1973, p. 13.
7. Tom Peters, *Thriving on Chaos* (Knopf, pp. 519–521).
8. Ron Willingham, *Integrity Selling* (Doubleday, p. 87).
9. Prov. 16:33.
10. Gen. 3:6.
11. 2 Sam. 11:2–4.
12. Charles R. Swindoll, *Come Before Winter and Share My Hope* (Living Books/Tyndale, p. 469).

13. Col. 3:5.

14. Luke 12:15.

15. Deut. 24:16.

16. Rom. 6:23.

17. Jas. 1:15.

18. Deut. 1:21.

19. Deut. 31:8.

20. Josh. 1:9.

21. Francis Schaeffer, *Joshua and the Flow of Biblical History* (InterVarsity Press, pp. 112–113).

22. Francis Schaeffer, *Joshua and the Flow of Biblical History* (InterVarsity Press, p. 121).

23. Prov. 14:34.

Chapter 7: The Peril of Prayerlessness

1. Matt. 10:16.

2. Acts 20:29–30.

3. Carl Armerding, *The Fight for Palestine* (Van Kampen Press, pp. 91–92).

4. Eph. 6:11.

5. F. B. Meyer, *Joshua: And the Land of Promise* (Revell, pp. 103–104).

6. F. B. Meyer, *Joshua: And the Land of Promise* (Revell, pp. 108).

7. Prov. 12:19.

8. Psalm 15:1–2,4.

9. "The Miracle of the Fog," *Good News Publisher.*

10. Rom. 8:31.

11. Daniel 11:32.

Chapter 8: Vanquishing Enemies

1. Charles R. Swindoll, *Come Before Winter and Share My Hope* (Living Books/Tyndale, pp. 208–209).

2. Psalm 20:7.

3. A. J. Mattill, Jr., "Universalism and the Conquest of Canaan," *Concordia Theological Monthly*, 35:1, pp. 8–17, January 1964.

4. *Perspective*, Sept. 28, 1977.

5. Henry T. Sell, *Bible Study by Periods* (Revell, p. 83).

6. Gal. 6:9.

7. Harvey Mackay, *Swim with the Sharks Without Being Eaten Alive* (William Morrow & Co., p. 266).

Chapter 9: The Divine Realtor at Work

1. Peter F. Drucker, *People And Performance: The Best Of Peter Drucker On Management* (Harper's College Press, p. 55).

2. William Blaikie, *The Book of Joshua* (Hodder & Stoughton, pp. 253–254).

3. Matt. 6:19–21.

4. Deut. 1:36.

5. Alexander Maclaren, *Expositions of Holy Scripture*, Vol. 3, p. 162.

6. *His* Magazine, April 1980, p. 23.

7. Gene A. Getz, *Joshua* (Regal, p. 161).

8. Charles R. Swindoll, *Come Before Winter and Share My Hope (*Living Books/Tyndale, pp. 201–202).

9. H. Forbes Witherby, *The Book of Joshua* (Loizeaux, p. 188).

10. Francis Schaeffer, *Joshua and the Flow of Biblical History* (InterVarsity Press, pp. 157–158, 162).

11. *Amy Carmichael of Dohnavur* (F. Houghton, p. 366).

Chapter 10: God's Inheritance— No One Left Out

1. Arthur Holmes, *The Idea of a Christian College* (Eerdmans, p. 115).

2. Isa. 9:1–2.

3. William Blaikie, *The Book of Joshua* (Hodder & Stoughton, p. 332).

4. Heb. 6:18.

5. Deut. 33:10.

6. William Blaikie, *The Book of Joshua* (Hodder & Stoughton, p. 352).

7. 2 Tim. 2:13.

8. 2 Cor. 1:20.

Chapter 11: The Danger of Misjudging Motives

1. Francis Schaeffer, *Joshua and the Flow of Biblical History* (InterVarsity Press, p. 174).

2. Allan C. Emery, *A Turtle on a Fencepost* (Word Books, pp. 46–47).

3. Francis Schaeffer, *Joshua and the Flow of Biblical History* (InterVarsity Press, p. 175).

4. Prov. 6:9.

5. Francis Schaeffer, *Joshua and the Flow of Biblical History* (InterVarsity Press, p. 177).

6. John J. Davis, *Conquest and Crisis* (Baker, p. 87).

7. Matt. 18:15; see also verses 16–17.

8. Gal. 6:1.

9. Prov. 15:1.

Chapter 12: The Counsel of an Old Soldier

1. Ps. 44:3.

2. Matt. 6:24.

3. G. W. Butler, *The Lord's Host* (William Oliphant, p. 322).

4. *Perspective*, April 8, 1980.

5. A *suzerain* is a nation which exercises control over

another nation; the nation which is so controlled is called a *vassal.*

6. Deut. 15:15, KJV.

7. Francis Schaeffer, *Joshua and the Flow of Biblical History* (InterVarsity Press, p. 206).

8. Joy Davidson, *Smoke on the Mountain* (The Westminster Press, pp. 30–31).

Note to the Reader

The publisher invites you to share your response to the message of this book by writing Discovery House Publishers, P. O. Box 3566, Grand Rapids, MI 49501, U.S.A. or by calling 1-800-653-8333. For information about other Discovery House publications, contact us at the same address and phone number.

Notes